## DEDICATION

I dedicate this book to the loving memory of Rita Mahimaidoss and Ammachi (my grandmother). This book acknowledges their spiritual presence in my life. This book is also dedicated to my loving husband who has been my source of strength at all times.

# CONTENTS

## Preface

The aim of this book is to help understand life better. Every incident narrated in this book is true and meant to prove that life is very meaningful and beautiful in spite of its pitfalls. It is also meant to help people who are tossed about, by the vicissitudes of life understand that God has a plan for every one of us. He never leaves us or forsakes us.

This book confirms the presence of our Angels and Spirit Guides who are there with us always, irrespective of circumstances.

Cover photo credits- Luke Michael and Jonatan Pie from Unsplash.

I sincerely thank Balachandar S for his cover design.

# GOD HAS OUR BACKS

ROSALINE BOSCO MAHIMAIDOSS

# CHAPTER I

## ANGELS OF GOD

Do you believe in Angels? If you do, how often have they been there for you? I was taught to believe in Angels, because my parents were Catholics and they raised me in the Catholic tradition. And I believed my parents.

My most unforgettable dream, which still remains detailed vividly in my memory, is about a host of Angels. They were gathered in a circle, close to the ceiling, exactly as I had seen them in Christmas cards. They were 'glorious' and were multi colored. They had lovely wings and were small. Their hands were folded in prayer and their heads bowed in reverence for their Creator. I became convinced about the Angels. I must have been three years old.

What does a three year old know about the world and what it has to offer? My innocence brought me the vision of the Angels that I still remember today. How did I lose them on my way? Do you have your angel with you still? Then you must be a lucky person, with a lot of determination. Because life takes you on bumpy rides, and it's easy to drop your Angels as you go by. And it's easier to stop believing in them.

Probably we are all raised with the expectation that 'Life is beautiful.' Yes. It is true. Life is beautiful. We think that beautiful means a 'trouble free' zone where there is only joy with no problems at all. I am sure that nobody would like to believe that problems are a part of life. That would be pessimistic according to the standards of the world.

Would we like to bring up our children with the thought that pain and problems are a part of life? Why is it essential for children to be brought up with the idea that things might go wrong sometimes?

Because, they will be strong and protected if they know what is ahead of them. They will not 'break down' during times of adversity. They will not crumble down like paper men or topple down like a pack of cards. They will know that life is definitely not a 'bed of roses,' but more of a 'roller coaster ride,' and the good and bad happen in rotation. But life still remains beautiful. That's when you start believing in Angels once more.

My story is about how I met my 'lost' Angels again. My wish for you is that you stay secure and close to your Angels and listen to them under all circumstances, because they only have your best interests at heart.

## CHAPTER II

### AN UNEXPECTED TWIST

I had turned seventeen. My childhood was a very normal one with nothing extraordinary. But it was very happy. I cannot say that I was pampered much as a child, but I had a completely joyous childhood. In fact I was a 'tomboy' and enjoyed playing with children of my age and also with children who were much younger than me. These children looked up to me because I organized games for them every day. I grew up believing that I did not have a care in the world.

Every evening after five, the children of the street would gather at my house to play. There was a long cemented platform in front of our house, and coconut trees on either side, where we regularly played Shuttlecock, Cricket and Catching game. We would even devise our own games and make rules for playing them. In fact, the residents of the street were very close, because of this bond of friendship formed by the children.

We would also play an indoor game called Trade which was quite popular when I was young. It was a great experience to trade countries for plastic coins. We would feel very important, as if we really owned the countries that we traded. We were always reluctant to go back home after playtime. My only brother played cricket with his friends. My cousin once remarked that the street had almost become lifeless since I left my hometown after my wedding.

In fact I was so much engrossed with my own world that I was not even aware that my mother was very ill, much beyond our family's worst expectations. It was at this time that I noticed that my parents had some conversations, which somehow seemed very secretive. They would excuse themselves and go to the terrace to have these conversations. It was later that I realized that they were discussing my wedding. But they had never mentioned this topic to me ever before, and so it was the last thing that was on my mind.

The idea of marriage did not register fully in my head. I just took it for granted that it was too far from becoming a reality. But it did. I was married at eighteen. The prime years of my life which should have been dedicated to my education, were taken over by the duties of becoming the mother of a beautiful baby girl, by the time I was nineteen.

In fact one of my household help once remarked that I wasn't even very skilled in holding my baby during that time. But my love for my baby gave me enough courage to take care of her. I lived far away from Madras, my home town where my parents worked. Probably, if communication facilities had been as advanced as they are now, I might have been happier. I would have called my mother frequently over the phone. It would have definitely helped me to understand her health condition better.

My mother was a teacher at a private school. She was a very pious woman who never harmed a soul. She had to travel for four hours to work every day. It became essential for her to work, because my parents had borrowed some loans to build a nice house in the city where we lived, called Madras.

My Father worked for the Government, known as the Secretariat. He was a senior officer, a dedicated staff member, and a person of much integrity. He was not a very expressive man, but the most loving father in the world. My brother was doing his 'Engineering' course in a College which was about four hundred miles away.

There was a reason why my mother planned to get me married early. She had worked as a teacher in a private school for thirty three years, and had completely dedicated her life to the school where she taught 'Tamil' the language of our State. All her energy and her life had been focused in this area. Working continuously for thirty three years in exacting conditions had taken its toll on her. She would often remark that she did not want me to see me suffer as she did.

It was not as if she did not love her profession. On the contrary, she loved it so much that she was unwilling to give it up, even after she became seriously sick. My mother's forebodings turned right, as she became seriously ill and had to be admitted in a hospital in the neighborhood. This was after my marriage. The experience is still a raw wound in my memory because of the unprofessional manner in which the doctors of the hospital treated her. They were mercenary.

They did not care much about an aged couple, who belonged to the middle income group. My mother had developed severe pain in her left leg by this time and the doctors did not know that it was due to the cancer in her intestine. They were unable to make a proper diagnosis and operated her leg. In addition to the excruciating pain, her leg was amputated due to faulty diagnosis. Our family was hit by financial as well as other difficulties. Life became miserable.

During this period I lived in a small town close to Vellore, taking care of my own family. My husband was a very active Professor in a 'Salesian' College. To be truthful, I could not help much, except feel sorrow for my parents who were such simple and kind people.

My constant regret was that they did not deserve to experience anything that had happened to them. I felt very guilty for not being able to take care of my mother. This guilt feeling was reduced only after I was able to take care of my father, later in life.

# CHAPTER III

## SMALL THINGS BRING THE GREATEST HAPPINESS

My *Ammachi* (Grandmother) was a widow and she played a major role in bringing us up. She was the embodiment of 'charisma' and a woman of great piety. Every morning she would wake up at five, and walk up the stairs to our house and help my mother prepare food. My mother would then pack lunches for all of us. She had stayed with my uncle's family after her retirement.

My maternal uncle and his family lived in the same house as we did. They lived on the ground floor. My four cousins were my best friends when I was young. They are still very special to me and we share a very special relationship, untarnished by events or the passage of time.

*Ammachi* had become a widow very early in life, when she was twenty eight years old. She had faced much adversity after widowhood in trying to make ends meet. Because of her hard work and resilient nature she was successful in educating her four children. All her children became trained teachers. It was fortunate that *Ammachi* had a lot of talents. She could draw well, make dresses and bags. She was able to bring up her children well. Her proficiency in Drawing and Arts and Crafts was what enabled her to become a teacher.

She had a meager widow's pension and she made dolls, sold saris, and even tried her hand at rearing chicken. She never believed in being idle. I remember that she bred huge chickens, some of which weighed even three kilograms. She had built a small room to raise the chickens close to our compound wall.

There was a huge demand for the chicken from the neighboring houses. During Christmas and other festivals she prepared delicious chicken gravy for us. She gave up the venture after some time because the hens developed infections, and it was becoming increasingly difficult for her to take care of them.

I still like to believe that I was one of her favorite granddaughters. I suppose her other granddaughters too thought the same. She was a source of strength at all times.

My father and mother worked hard to give us more than what they could afford, and did not deprive us of a good education. We were educated in the best Schools and Colleges in the city. We were lucky to enjoy delicious meals prepared by the loving hands of my mother and *Ammachi*. We would have a simple breakfast of *Idlis* (a steamed round shaped eatable made with rice batter and black gram), or Bread and Butter with a generous helping of Jam. Our packed lunch would usually be rice with *Sambhar* (dal with vegetables and spices), with boiled eggs and a vegetable to school. *Chappathis* and *Puris* (made with wheat dough) were special items that we savored during the weekends.

After she returned from work in the evenings, my mother would prepare some fish curry or fried fish as an accompaniment to eat with rice. My brother excelled in his studies. While I loved Literature, he scored very good marks in all his exams and qualified to be an Engineer. My parents were naturally very proud of him

I believed that our family of four was the happiest in the world, and would have challenged anybody who dared to contradict me. Every Sunday, we would accompany *Ammachi* to the church which was about two miles away, but we never minded the distance. The roads were not very crowded those days, unlike today.

Now a bustling metro has sprung up on the way to the church, and it has become one of the busiest areas in the city. Going to the church was a special occasion, and we wore beautiful clothes every Sunday. We did not go out much and this was an 'outing' that we looked forward to.

We would walk happily gazing at the wayside shops. Sundays was a very busy for the shop keepers. People would throng the mutton and chicken stalls which were on the sides of the streets. In fact walking to the church was more enjoyable and captivating to the senses than sitting through the long service and sermon, especially for a child like me. What I liked best about the Church service were the beautiful hymns that were sung to praise God. Listening to these hymns was very uplifting to the spirit and made me feel that I was in heaven with God and his Angels.

My mother was very particular that we should pray fervently. I usually sat with my eyes fixed on the priest who was offering the mass, and prayed for God's mercy, throughout the service. We were never allowed to talk while the service was going on. My mother was very strict and made sure that we were brought up in a pious manner.

We had to follow every gesture of the priest and respond to the prayers without fail. Though I had a reasonably good voice, I never had the courage to join the Church choir. This was because I suffered from an 'inferiority' complex. I believed that I was not as well dressed or as smart as the members of the choir. So I felt shy to join the choir even though I would have loved to do so.

My mother always encouraged me to sing all the hymns from our seats. Since we attended mass early in the morning, it was always an English service. I was very familiar with the songs sung in our church. It was a Catholic church.

A majority of the choir members were from Kerala, and had no qualms about wearing pants and beautiful tops. Most of them had short cropped hairstyles. I thought that they were really brave and smart to do so. To my eyes, they seemed very exquisite and glamorous. They seemed to have an ethereal quality about them. They appeared very elegant and I would look at them with awe and admiration.

Though we were always neatly dressed, we never wore fancy clothes as they did. This admiration for clothes probably had an impact on my dressing style as a young woman, and I bought more clothes than was necessary, after I began to work. The *saris* in my wardrobe were of all hues and textures and I would fold them neatly, arrange them on the shelves of my 'Almirah' and admire their softness with my hands whenever I had the time. It was one of my favorite hobbies.

I had hundreds of *saris,* and though I gave away many to the maids who worked for me, I still retain some very beautiful ones. But this practice of buying s*aris* stopped after I preferred to take a voluntary retirement from my job, as an Assistant Professor in a College.

*Ammachi* was my Guardian Angel in my childhood and she would appear miraculously whenever I needed her. One remarkable incident of this kind happened, when I was about eight or nine years old.

The cooking gas cylinder in our house had become empty. I decided to make tea and prepared to light a Kerosene stove. Since cylinders were in great demand then, everybody had Kerosene stoves. I tried pouring the Kerosene into the small hole in the stove, without realizing that the liquid had spilled all around the stove. I was on the verge of lighting it, just as *Ammachi* entered the house.

I now realize that it was a *synchronicity* and not a *coincidence* that she entered the house at the right moment. This realization is more pronounced, especially now, after I have experienced a lot of *synchronicities* happening at various points of my life. If not for her presence, the stove would have burst the second it was lighted, as I had spilled kerosene all over and around it.

Since my mother was working, it was *Ammachi* who helped me to take care of my baby girl as soon as she was born. She would wake up on hearing my baby cry and in turn wake me up to feed her. Every day, for almost a month she prepared special varieties of food that strengthened a woman after childbirth. She would make different kinds of fish curries with black pepper, and with very little spice. These dishes were easily digestible and tasty too, as they were prepared with much love.

Christmas season was heavenly with my *Ammachi* teaming up with my mother to make cakes, *badhushas* (a soft melting sweet made out of all purpose flour and ghee), *adhirasams* (made with rice flour and jaggery), *laddus* (a sweet made with gram flour), *Murukku* (a crunchy savory made from rice flour) and other mouth watering delicacies.

*Ammachi* always made two varieties of cakes, plum and sponge. We would make a small 'crib' every year. My mother would send us to every neighbor's house in the street to give them the home made delicacies. These delicacies were neatly arranged in a long ever-silver tray.

The tray was always covered with a green scarf. We were overjoyed to be received by our neighbors with our simple but tasty offerings. I still remember running up and down the staircase to perform this errand. The green scarf was washed and kept clean and used regularly for this purpose. It seemed to carry the Christmas 'aura' around it. The joy of Christmas is in sharing, and we felt very happy about it. Almost all the neighbors in the street were Hindus. They reciprocated by giving us homemade delicacies during Diwali, the festival of lights.

We enjoyed celebrating Diwali as much as we enjoyed celebrating Christmas. We would pester our parents to buy us crackers and sparklers and would eagerly wait for the day that my father brought the crackers home. Then we would pounce on them and distribute them equally between ourselves. I would never allow my brother to have an extra share. He was more daring, and would get more crackers and I would have more sparklers. There was a competition among our friends in the street about who would burst more crackers every year.

Usually my brother would finish all his crackers quickly and beg me for more. But I usually did not give him any of mine. Such was our love for bursting crackers. The left over crackers (if there were any) would be saved for Christmas.

The love that *Ammachi* had for my mother was unconditional and my mother reciprocated through small acts of gratitude towards her. One among the long list of *Ammachi's* hobbies was selling *saris*. She sold *saris* which could be worn by working women. These *saris* were very beautiful and were multi colored. She would travel to the end of the city to the wholesale market and buy *saris* in bulk, so that she could make a minimum profit from the sale.

She never sold for much profit. She would discuss the prices of these *saris* with my mother. Then she would write them on small pieces of paper, and pin them to the *saris*. My mother carried them to the school where she worked, and because they were very reasonably priced, there was a demand for the *saris* from her colleagues.

My mother too had a reasonable number of *saris* which she wore, neatly draped around her body, to school every day. These *saris* were very beautiful because she had an eye for colors. She also had in-skirts of the same color which were worn underneath. The *sari* was pleated neatly and tucked inside the skirt.

It requires patience to drape a *sari* neatly and to keep it in place. It is also quite risky for an amateur to tuck the *sari* into the skirt, and perform daily activities, because there is always a danger of the pleats becoming loose, and the *sari* coming down. So the pleats are usually secured with a safety pin or a brooch, to the blouse near the shoulder. Nowadays women use a lot of safety pins to keep the *sari* in position because they do not wear saris regularly, and find it difficult to do so.

I was always enamored by the colorful *saris* and tried them on when my mother wasn't around. The lovely *saris* were my mother's prized acquisitions. She did not buy jewels or cosmetics for herself because she considered it as wasteful expenditure. She would rather buy jewels for me. Now, I have a huge collection of dresses and *saris* that I have accumulated over the years. But, I cannot buy one for my mother.

In spite of selling *saris* I never remember Ammachi wearing beautiful clothes, or being dressed very grandly. She wore very simple cotton *saris* most of the time, and wore white *saris* to church. This was purely out of her own volition, because there was nobody to criticize her if she had chosen to dress in colorful clothes. In fact, I never remember her wearing jewels on any occasion.

Since I had young children (my baby boy was born by the year 1988), I was not able to take care of my mother during the last stages of her life. *Ammachi* nursed my mother throughout the various stages of her cancer, until she passed away in 1990. My son was about two years old and I could not entrust him to anybody's care. I was not able to stay in Madras, because my daughter attended school in the town where we lived.

My father had not yet retired when she was critically ill, and he had to continue to work for meeting the medical expenses. He would visit her every day after work, and rush to see her in the hospital every morning. *Ammachi* was always beside her daughter's bedside in all her moments of suffering. It is the greatest agony for a mother to tolerate. She had to bear witness to her daughter's suffering.

As my mother's disease progressed to its final stages, *Ammachi* developed some resentment towards my father. Probably she held him accountable for my mother's illness. She believed that my mother developed cancer because she had overworked for the sake of her family. I knew that it was *Ammachi's* love for her daughter that created this kind of angst.

My mother had always found satisfaction in her teaching profession and was reluctant to give it up. She gave up her job only after her health became so worse, that she could not continue working.

In spite of all the agonies that *Ammachi* faced in her life, she never questioned the presence of God. There was acceptance for every suffering as the 'will' of God. Such was the unshakeable trust which she had in God, that she never uttered a single word of complaint against the brutal conditions of life. Besides, she was so busy in acquiring new skills and practicing them, that she never actually had the time to grumble about anything.

These qualities were also reflected in her four children, my mother, my aunts and my uncle who followed their mother's footsteps meticulously. I grew up without yearning for anything extraordinary. I was perfectly happy in the company of my parents and *Ammachi*, who loved me unconditionally.

## CHAPTER IV

### THE FIRST JUDGMENT

Our school was located at a different part of the city from where we lived. My brother and I had to travel quite a long distance to reach our schools. We travelled for almost four hours every day. The bus would stop at almost twenty different places on its way to my school. As soon as a few people alighted from the bus, many more would board it. So the buses were always crowded.

Since our schools were in a thriving part of the city, and our parents could not afford to buy a big house close to where the schools were located, we had settled closer to the suburbs. This made it very tiresome for us to travel to and from our schools. My brother sometimes fell asleep in the bus, while returning home from school and missed his stop. He would then travel back in another bus to reach home.

My mother worked in an 'Anglo Indian Boys School' and since my school was very close, I regularly went to my mother's school to eat my lunch. Her colleagues shared their food among themselves and I was very fond of the 'meat cutlet' that one of the Anglo Indian teachers used to bring.

My mother too prepared tasty fish cutlets with *Kanangeluthi* (Mackerel) fish and the taste still lingers in my mouth. The cutlet had an equal ratio of fish and potatoes and was very crunchy and flavorsome. She also added coriander leaves and green chilies to the cutlet dough. The whole house would be filled with the aroma of the fish cutlets and our lunch would be eaten very quickly and without complaint.

She worked in a school called Dominic Savio. Whenever my school closed early; I used to spend time playing in the vast premises of the school where my mother worked.

There is a Cathedral on the same road where her school was located and every day, immediately after alighting from the bus, my mother would walk across the road to go to the Church, and offer her prayers for all her loved ones. This Church is built on the mortal remains of one of the twelve apostles of Jesus Christ, St. Thomas. After her daily supplication she would proceed to her school. She was very much loved and appreciated by the students for her teaching skills and affectionate nature.

Since she was a very soft spoken woman and very sensitive, she was easily hurt by people who were not so kind in their words and deeds. I decided early in my life, that I would not to be trod upon by unkind people, or hurt by the rudeness of others. Instead I decided that I would deal with people as they deserved to be treated, so that I did not get hurt in the process. I felt that it was my right to be treated with dignity, in spite of the opinions and judgments of others.

When my classes were over I would play games with my friends and then leave school. My school had vast playgrounds and since it was administered by the 'Franciscan Nuns, it had a very fine chapel. We would admire the church bell which was massive. We would climb up the steep stairs to have a closer look at the bell, which seemed to have a magical quality about it.

'Catechism' was a part of the curriculum for Christian students and others were taught 'Moral Science.' The Hindu students were as enthusiastic in visiting the chapel as we were. They were not prejudiced against other religions. They would recite the morning prayers including the 'Our Father' with much gusto.

This is one quality among the Hindu brethren that I admire the most. A person needs to be very mature and tolerant to respect the beliefs of people belonging to other religions. Because of their positive attitude, I would visit temples when we went on tours from our school.

Some of my friends would refuse to enter Hindu temples but I thought that it was a very mean and a petty attitude. I acquired this quality from my father. Although he was a very staunch Catholic, he respected the beliefs of people who belonged to other religions.

After returning from my mother's school post lunch, I would play with my friends until the bell rang once more to summon us into the class rooms. I was not very interested in Mathematics. These classes filled me with terror. My teacher was very strict, and was particular that the students should submit their homework the next day without fail. Each of us had our own desks at school. I would hide under the huge desk and escape from her eyes. I was about ten years old then.

She would call the shirkers and ask them to extend their hands and beat them with her long wooden scale. I was terrified of her. I don't remember being so afraid of any other teacher in the school. But to my surprise, I was able to score eighty percent in Mathematics during my tenth grade. I think the fear of Mathematics was my undoing and that was what made matters worse. So, in spite of being offered the 'Science' stream which was considered to be more meritorious I opted for the 'Arts' stream for my Higher Secondary education.

This gleaning from the past reminds me that we, with our minds, create our own monsters. The fears that we nurture, grow into gigantic proportions just like 'Jack's Beanstalks' and prevent us from reaching our highest potentials.

One of the most attractive places in the school was the Library. I practiced the skill of reading a story book right under the teacher's nose. Still, I knew that all teachers could not be so easily hoodwinked. But I was so besotted with books that I could not resist the temptation of reading books, even while I was eating.

My parents would reprimand me saying, 'Pay attention to your meals as it will not do you any good to do two things at the same time,' but I never took their words seriously. It was this love for books which made me choose Literature as my major subject, for my Graduate and Post Graduate studies. Books are fascinating for children as they transport them to the world of fantasy even beyond their wildest dreams. It is unfortunate that this wonderful world is losing its luster for the young, because of the invasion of substitutes.

Money holds a special fascination for children because it can be bartered for things that they love the most, like colored candies, gums and toys. Nowadays, parents make sure that their children get more than what they desire and feel gratified. But parents of an older generation believed in the maxim, 'Spare the rod and spoil the child,' and strictness was considered to be a virtue. My parents were very vigilant in this regard, and made sure that we followed all the dictates of our religion. But what would a six year old know about these, when the jingling of coins in her hand meant more candies and chewing gum.

My mother carried a Black Hand bag to school every day. She did not have a collection of bags as we do these days, but was content with one. She just carried whatever was essential for her to teach at school, in her bag. Carrying cosmetics was unheard of, especially to a middle class working woman, who was always short of time.

One compartment of the bag had blue and red ink pens. The blue pen was for signing her attendance, and the red for marking notebooks. The last compartment of her bag carried a lot of 'change' for buying bus tickets, as the conductors demanded exact change from travelers. Sometimes they were outright rude to a person who did not carry the exact change for buying a ticket.

The last compartment of my mother's bag was very appealing to me. My childish imagination was fired with the thought of the hundreds of candies I could buy with all that jingling money. One day I could not resist my temptation any longer, and I grasped a handful of coins from her bag and took them to school. That was probably the happiest day of my childhood.

My father had escorted my brother and me to a movie titled, 'Willie Wonka and the Chocolate Factory,' when we were children. This was a movie about a candy factory. I was wonder struck with the fountains and rivers which emitted soft drinks and chocolates. I fell in love with the movie.

It was as if this fantasy had come true and I was suddenly able to buy all the candies in the world. I was ecstatic and bought all the candies I wanted. There was a canteen close to the entrance of the school which sold these items, and was very popular among the students. As soon as the bell rang for lunch, we would rush to the canteen to buy the multi colored sweets displayed attractively in huge glass bottles. There was also a store right in front of our school called 'Orient Stores.'

The name of the store is still fresh on my mind because of the 'grape' ice cream that was sold there. I don't think there was any student in our school who did not love that flavor. The ice cream also had some grapes thrown here and there for authenticity.

The ice cream and a unique chocolate wrapped in golden paper were all I bought from the store. This chocolate was shaped like a coin. I think these chocolates which are very tempting to children, are still available in the market. During exams we would buy sheets of paper and stationery items from the store.

We did not have too many choices for buying the goodies. We had to choose either the school canteen or 'Orient Stores.' My favorite chewing gum was available in the canteen. It was pink in color when unwrapped, and the taste was incredible. But what was more attractive was that if you opened the wrapper to find a white colored gum, you could claim another one for free. I remember spending a lot of money on these bubble gums as we called them. But this stolen pleasure did not last for a long time.

I do not remember the length of time that I enjoyed the unlimited candies, but I was shocked when I saw my mother walking into my school one day, and she 'caught me' in the act. Though I was very young, I remember the shame associated with being scolded by my mother, before my friends, even today. She had been missing a lot of coins and had found out that I was the culprit.

She was perfectly justified in wanting to bring up her daughter as a good person. This incident has stayed with me always as it is associated with the feeling of embarrassment that I faced at school. I should reiterate that my mother's love for me did not decrease. I knew that she loved me more than herself and it must have broken her heart to think that her daughter would not fit into the standards prescribed by society and religion. I must have been in the second or the third standard when this incident occurred. I have freed myself of the judgment now. I know that it was the fantasy of a young child enamored by candies.

Another judgment that I faced as a child, is related to the dresses I wore to school. My *Ammachi* stitched most of my frocks and dresses. She was an expert at tailoring and stitched beautiful dresses for me. But I missed wearing 'ready made' frocks. We had a mixture of students belonging to the middle class and the rich at school. My friends wore attractive clothes on their birthdays, and I was fascinated by their dresses. I was waiting for an opportunity to wear a beautiful dress to school, and become an object of admiration.

I was very happy when my mother bought me a dress which was quite exotic. The top was pink and it had floral designs. The pants were a subtle plain pink. I was waiting for the right occasion to wear it. Sometimes, on very special occasions, we were allowed to wear colored dresses to school. The Principal made this announcement during the 'Assembly' and it was welcomed very enthusiastically by the children.

I was waiting for this day and it arrived. We were asked to wear colored dresses the next day. I decided to show off my new dress to my class mates. I wore it with pride and eagerness, sure that it would be appreciated.

My happiness was short lived. I heard one of my classmates say to another, 'She must really have guts to wear that dress.' The dress was not a revealing one to elicit this comment. Her meaning was very clear. She had never seen me wear pretty dresses and had concluded that I was not supposed to do so. This remark stayed in my mind forever, emphasizing the fact that some judgments we receive during our early years, leave an indelible mark in our hearts. I must have been eight years old at that time.

It is imperative that children should be judged and criticized with caution, according to their age and maturity levels, and one standard for all may not be beneficial in the long run. Parents should pay attention to the vulnerabilities of their children and try to address them suitably. This will help a child grow without complexes.

# CHAPTER V

## THE MIRACLE OF LIFE

My little angel had grown up and was going to school. Dropping her at school and coming back to finish my daily chores was my only responsibility, and the days were growing arduous and wearisome. I was still a teenager and very energetic. I wanted some purpose in life. I also longed for a sense of achievement. Our house was within a huge compound where there were two more houses. It was a rented house. One of the houses was occupied by the Landlord's family. A young couple lived in the other house.

The couple was mostly dressed in white. The wife was accustomed to wearing crisp white cotton *saris*. These *saris* were dipped in starch and ironed neatly so that they remained stiff until the end of the day. The pleats of the *saris* she wore stood straight and neat, and gave her a very dignified look. She was a working woman.

How I wished I could also go to work! Alas! I hadn't completed my degree course and it was not possible to get work, unless I was qualified with a basic degree. My husband suggested that I should complete my degree through a Correspondence Course. He supported me unconditionally. I started attending weekend sessions for my BA English Literature course. I loved studying Literature. Poetry was my favorite area of study. Since I had a passion for my course of study, I passed with very good credits and decided to apply for a job.

I could not apply to reputed institutions as they demanded a Bachelor's degree in Education. I applied for the post of an English teacher at a school which was not very demanding about a degree in 'Education.' I was asked to conduct a trial session for the students of standard eight. The young girls had their heads covered and I could only see their eyes. I could see their slippers though. Every one of them wore exotic slippers as though to compensate for covering their beautiful clothes.

I could also see a bit of their clothing which was very rich and fanciful. Their eyes revealed a lot of interest in studying. They were excited, when they heard me speak fluently, and without hesitation. I liked the students very much. They were full of joy and life. I knew that they liked me too. Their appreciation brought a sense of fulfillment which I had been longing for. Though I had no experience in teaching, my passion for this profession made up for my inadequacy. The management too was highly satisfied with my skills.

After the demonstration, I was called before the committee members for an interview. They questioned me until they were completely satisfied, and the matter of salary was discussed. I later realized that they had expected me to demand a higher salary than what I had asked for, and were ready to pay it. But they had to conceal their surprise when I asked for less than what I deserved.

My anxiety to be placed in a job was so high, that I literally undersold myself. I do not regret the decision I made at that time.

I was almost desperate for a job, because I knew it was the only remedy for my boredom. I loved my first job and my encounter with the 'little ones.'

The 'Kindergarten' was my favorite class to teach, as the joy of the children that I met there, was unbridled and without reservations. Since I taught English, I had to teach many classes beginning from the Kindergarten to High School. There was also a boy's section in the same school and it faced the opposite direction of the girls' section.

The boys were very rebellious and they had to be dealt with, in a tough manner. The management also made it clear that the students should be disciplined at 'any cost'. I had to fall in line with their expectations. I was able to manage the classes without resorting to violence. The students loved me wholeheartedly and I too loved them unconditionally. I worked in this school for two years.

I had the opportunity to wear all the colorful *saris* that I had stacked in my wardrobe. My colleagues wondered and remarked at my *saris*. They remarked that I must have at least three hundred and sixty five *saris* to wear throughout the year. It was not completely true. But I had a lot of *saris*, indeed too many. I felt happy with their generous compliments. Their positive remarks seemed to afford me the satisfaction that I had missed during my school days.

It was during this time that a Professor who was also my husband's colleague visited us. He had heard about my mother from the head of a reputed institution in the locality. He also presented lectures during my weekly sessions at the 'Open University' where I studied. He was impressed with my assignments.

He advised me to submit an application to another reputed institution in the locality. His suggestion changed the course of my life. It was a *synchronicity* that the Professor had heard of my deceased mother, who had been such an excellent teacher.

After my mother's death, I always prayed to her. Nobody told me to do so. I felt that it was completely right to pray to her, because I knew that she was a pure soul. I was not wrong. She always heard my prayer and interceded to God on my behalf.

God endows good souls, with power to help us. We should trust in them. Many incidents that occurred in my life later are also proof to the fact, that our spirit guides are always with us, and they help us in times of need or despair. But we need the faith to reach out to them.

Meanwhile, I had to say goodbye to the school that I loved so much, and the students who were very friendly with me were very sad. Some of them asked me why I had to leave them, and I could not give a convincing answer. I felt that their eyes were accusing me of deserting them. The members of the management were also quite sorry to lose me.

They offered me a higher salary and tried to convince me to stay there, but I knew that I could not enrich my learning and experience if I decided to stay there. In spite of my sadness, I remained unwavering in my decision to leave. To this day I remember shedding tears, while leaving the school, which gave me hope.

The school gave me the confidence of being financially independent. I did not like to be dependent on my husband for my every need. It also endowed me with self confidence, which is essential for a woman. I enjoyed buying books and clothes for my family, with my salary.

The new school was very huge and it was run by a religious Congregation. Another interesting fact was that, this school had never employed a lady teacher before, and it was a novel experience for the students to have a 'lady' teacher (as I was frequently referred to).

I did not work full time but was engaged as a 'part time' teacher until I proved my worth. I had been working for almost a month when I noticed something strange. I had a room for myself in the first storey of the school building. Sometimes I would go home for lunch and return back to school for the afternoon sessions. I would leave my bag behind since I did not want to carry it for a short while and because I did not carry any money in my bag.

One afternoon, when I returned back from lunch, I noticed that my red pen which I used for marking my students' class work, was removed from my bag, and kept in a different place. I realized that somebody wanted me to notice the displacement. I dismissed this event as the trick of a prankster, and went about my tasks in the usual manner.

This strange event kept repeating itself very often and I would find the contents of my bag replaced in very strange places in the room. Meanwhile I also noticed that a student was always following me with his eyes and was trying to make 'eye contact.' He was a new comer to the school. I would suddenly encounter him lurking in corners, and in unexpected places.

I did not connect these two happenings and ignored the 'gawking' student. This seemed to have sparked a lot of animosity in the boy. I later understood that he had wanted to have a conversation with me but did not have the courage to do so, since I had been so elusive.

Things went on as usual and I was happy to teach in the new school which had better infra-structure. The management insisted that teachers should organize a lot of 'extracurricular' activities for the students. So we were always busy with a lot of activities.

The school kept me busy and happy. Days passed and Sports Day was imminent. The days before the Sports day were looked forward to, with a lot of expectation by the students. They spent a lot of time in the vast playgrounds practicing for the great day.

One morning as it was my habit, I remained in the staff room marking corrections in the composition notes of the students. There was not a soul in the classrooms, as all the students had left to the playground for various practices. The school had long corridors which stretched from one end to the other. I could see the empty looming corridors, from where I sat facing them, on my chair. It gave me a slight sense of unease.

The room which had originally been a library had been converted to accommodate me. It had very tall French windows which almost touched the ceiling, befitting an old school. These windows had screens which touched the floor, and I never bothered to draw the curtains aside when I entered the room, since I did not stay there for a long time. On that eventful day too I had not bothered to draw the curtains aside. The room was quite dark and just had enough light, to allow me to mark the note books.

I was bending over my note books fully concentrating on my work when it happened. There was not the slightest sound or movement but I believe that it was just my 'Angel' who alerted me. I looked behind me to see the 'gawking' student behind me, standing with an iron rod in his hand. He had come out surreptitiously from his hiding place. He had hidden behind a long curtain ingeniously, and had waited for me to concentrate fully on my work, before coming out of his hiding place. This curtain was behind the chair where I was sitting. His hand was uplifted and ready to come down strongly upon my head at any moment.

I do not know what force impelled me to run swiftly across the room, and down the stairs. But I did it instantaneously, in absolute fear for my life. Luckily the stairs were few in number. I reached the office, breathless and frightened, and informed the office- in- charge that I wanted to meet the Principal immediately. He looked at me quizzically but spoke to the Principal over the phone, and confirmed my appointment with him immediately.

The boy himself was in a state of 'shock,' as he had not expected me to turn behind and look into his eyes, at that exact moment that he had been ready to strike me. Otherwise he would have definitely struck me as planned. He stood rooted to the spot, unable to carry out his intention of striking me.

The culprit had dislodged a loose rod from a window. He had been planning to attack me for quite some time, and the deviousness of the plan overwhelmed me. Since I was a newly appointed to the school, the Principal questioned the student about the incident, first. Luckily he accepted his wrongdoing. If he had lied about what had happened, the situation might have turned against me.

I should admit that this incident scared me out of my wits for some time and I was relieved after another lady teacher was appointed in the school, the very next year. The student, unfortunately, had to continue his education elsewhere. He was also provided with counseling for his behavior.

Children who are sick either physically or mentally should be treated with care and concern. I was very sad that this incident had occurred and caused a disturbance in the life of a young boy. I later realized that this gave him a chance to reform himself. Otherwise he might have become a delinquent, and it would have scarred him for the rest of his life. I thanked my 'Angel' and my lucky stars for having escaped unscathed.

# CHAPTER VI

## THE SECOND JUDGMENT

In Indian society, one of the pre- requisites required for a girl before her wedding, is to learn the art of cooking. My mother had tried her best to get me involved in small tasks in the kitchen. She wanted me to become a proper 'housewife' after my marriage.

But I was not interested in cooking. I was more interested in reading. I was just above average in studies, but a very voracious reader. In fact I read everything that I set my eyes on, and my favorite haunt was a room in my uncle's house where there was a treasure of books.

I would just pick up a book and start reading it, and refuse to put it down until I completed it. I never remember asking for my uncle's permission before borrowing a book. I thought there was no need for me to learn to cook. There were two women to cook good wholesome meals for us, my mother and Ammachi.

Our family loved seafood, and every weekend my father would set off to the local market to buy fresh fish, caught from the sea. He usually bought enough fish to last us for a week. He always used his bicycle to go to the market. Since he was a regular customer, he would be welcomed warmly by the women who sold the fish.

They always gave him the best fish, since he was a soft spoken and well mannered gentleman, and did not bargain much. He never thought twice about paying a good sum for 'fresh' fish. He just bought us the best. The menu was decided based on the fish that he bought home.

If he bought Seer fish home, my mother prepared *Meen Kuzhambu* (fish curry) which is gravy made with tamarind extract, spices, onions, tomatoes, coconut and curry leaves. The gravy prepared by my mother was very tasty, and the delicious fish soaked in the gravy, would melt in our mouths.

She would also deep fry some of the fish slices in sizzling oil, after marinating them for a while in chilli- powder, turmeric powder and salt. Fried fish was our favorite, and we would relish every morsel of our food happily. The house work was divided in a fair measure between my parents, and I never noticed them complain about their work. We always had maids to wash clothes and clean the house.

My father bought fresh prawns frequently. It was my task to assist Ammachi in cleaning the prawns. She would spread an old newspaper on the floor and sit before it with the utensil which had the prawns. We chatted happily while working, and even while it was being cleaned I would imagine eating the fresh prawn gravy, garnished with plenty of onions, sautéed in oil, mixed with tomato puree and some spices. My mother added fennel seed powder to the gravy to enhance its flavor. Prawn curry was always a good accompaniment to rice. My brother and I adored it.

My mother made sure that we ate all our vegetables. She did not allow us to waste food or express dislike for vegetables. It was probably because of all the care lavished upon me that I had long hair.

*Ammachi* always came to my side after I washed my hair, and dry it tenderly with a towel. She would then light up frankincense with some pieces of charcoal and place it in a convenient position below my hair. *Ammachi* would then hold my hair gently, so that the warmth of the frankincense dried my hair quickly. I loved its fragrance.

She would dry my hair, conversing with my mother at the same time. This was done with so much love and care that I remember it as vividly as yesterday. I had to leave my small loving family after my wedding and missed Ammachi and my parents very badly.

Since my wedding happened suddenly, I was not trained in house hold or financial matters. My mother must have been very worried about how I would take care of my house after my wedding. But she never discussed it with me.

She kept all her longings locked inside her heart and did not confide her fears to me, probably because I was immature. My parents always protected me. They had never taught me that fate might strike a blow anytime. My mother did not tell me she was seriously sick. She wanted to protect me from grief, even though she suffered badly.

Bearing a child at nineteen is not extraordinary for an Indian woman. I tried to do as much justice as I could in taking care of my baby girl. My husband was always busy with his commitments at work. His friends' wives and his sisters performed their duties diligently, but all I had done was to read story books. I was not at all prepared for the daily chores.

The worst times were when my baby became sick due to infections. I would become terribly anxious and spend sleepless nights taking care of her. The small town did not boast of very good medical facilities but we took the children to a doctor couple who took care of minor ailments. They did not prescribe very strong antibiotics, which was the reason why we went to their clinic.

My children grew up into beautiful loving kids with their own identity, and as strong individuals who are capable of inspiring me.

Besides what they learned at school, I would give them additional coaching at home. I made sure that they studied their daily lessons. Meanwhile I had joined a correspondence course of study at 'IGNOU' which was an Open University. I had to attend classes every weekend. Assignments were given and marked by tutors of the College to which this University was affiliated. I found my mentors among two of these professors. They considered me as a good student. There were not many students who could write well, in that rural setting. I received a lot of encouragement and passed my UG Degree creditably.

One of these Professors gave me a reference, when I applied for the post of a teacher in the second school where I worked. My mother had passed away by then leaving me inconsolable.

All the sufferings that she underwent in spite of being a very pious and a good woman struck my heart very deeply and I was puzzled. My faith in God was shaken. I thought that God was cruel. My father and my brother were the worst affected. But I received a great blessing after her death.

My mother became my Angel after she left this world. It happened that, one of the Headmasters from the school where she had worked for thirty three years was transferred to the small town where I lived. He was friendly with the Professor who taught me at College, and spoke about my mother's dedicated service. In turn, my mentor spoke highly about me. I firmly believe that it was through my mother's intercession that I was placed as a teacher in the school. She gave me a reference even after her death.

'Ask and you shall receive,' is not an empty statement for those who believe it to be true. It might sound too *farfetched* for people who do not have such experiences. But these kinds of *synchronicities* continued throughout my life helping me at difficult times.

My mother always knew that I longed to complete my education, and I could feel her benign and healing presence always. I very strongly believe that the people who are very close to us never leave us spiritually, even though they might have left us physically.

In spite of becoming a working woman, braving all the odds that life dealt me with; I was still not considered to be a perfect cook. This was a matter bemoaned by my relatives who thought that I would never learn to cook a tasty meal in my life. I thought that this was a severe judgment passed on me, as I had learnt the art of cooking by then.

Sometimes, the gender roles assigned are very unreasonable as women are expected to work at home, as well as to fulfill their career roles. My husband was very supportive in this regard and we employed a cook. I should say that I was relieved by this measure and I was able to focus on completing my PG and M.Phil degrees.

Passing judgments is easy. Our actions and responses depend on the unique situations faced by us, according to our circumstances in life. Is it fair to underestimate ourselves based on the expectations of others? Judging ourselves based on other people's standards of measurement is not fair.

Judgments stifle our growth and make us feel worthless. Rising above these judgments, makes one strong and self confident. It ensures that we never give up on ourselves. God loves people who keep trying, in spite of facing failures and ridicule.

## CHAPTER VII

## SUPERNATURAL EXPERIENCES

Every mind is unique and has a different view of life. Creativity arises from being original. An individual's decisions and behavior is based on thousands of incidents that have happened right from the time that he is born. No two people's experiences can be the same. If we pay importance to others' judgments we will remain prisoners of their opinions forever. There is no need to worry even if we are not appreciated by human beings for what we do.

We can always rely on the support and guidance of our Angels. I was able to get this support from my deceased mother. With the passage of time I could feel the presence of my Angel through Clairaudience. I was very excited and not afraid at all at this new development.

Clairaudience is the supposed faculty of hearing, what is inaudible. I would hear a small object being moved very slightly in my vicinity. It would not be loud enough to frighten me, but was usually very low in volume, as if to reassure me. Not being a very courageous person, I was often surprised that these incidents did not frighten me out of my wits, but only created a sense of intrigue and reassurance.

Today there is a lot of research happening in the area of 'Near Death' studies. Anita Moorjani who was cured from cancer after her Near Death experience is an example of a person who came back to life after death. But there are thousands more who are objects of study.

These people have been interviewed thoroughly about their experiences. Almost all of them report that they passed through a 'Tunnel' immediately after their death. They were met by their spirit guides and received guidance from them. Then they inevitably meet the 'Light' or God. The process is methodical and there is no difference in the greeting that they received in Heaven, based on the differences practiced on Earth such as race, religion or status.

Scientists cannot claim that these people are hallucinating, because they clearly remembered happenings which occurred after they were 'clinically' pronounced to be dead. They were able to report the words that their physicians spoke, after their death.

All of them report that they were engulfed by the most wonderful loving feeling that cannot be experienced here, on Earth. They realized that they felt more 'at home' in heaven, than on earth. They met their close relatives who had passed away before them and their joy was boundless.

These survivors report that time did not happen in a linear fashion in Heaven, but the past, the present and the future happened at once. They had a 360 degree viewing capacity during this experience. They could see from all sides and be everywhere. Very few people who have been to heaven describe God as an avenger of sins. They reveal that God's judgment happens in a very loving manner.

Judgment was pronounced through a life review. All kind and good actions are reviewed favorably. Hurting others through words and actions is considered the most despicable offence in heaven, according to their reports. Some say that they had to relive the experience of those whom they offended or hurt.

This is literally equal to stepping into the 'shoes' of those whom we have wronged. It is reported to be a very vivid and a painful experience. The pain is not reported to be physical, but more related to the consciousness of the soul.

The colors in Heaven are reported to be so vivid that everything on Earth pales in comparison. The love experienced by these Near Death survivors was so infinite, that a majority of the survivors did not want to return to Earth after this experience. Everything was communicated telepathically in Heaven, and knowledge transmission was instantaneous, and all encompassing.

People who experienced Near Death felt shocked to see their own bodies, immediately after their death and realized later, that they were separated from their bodies. That is when they knew that they were dead. They were not allowed much time to speculate in this state. They were 'sucked' into the tunnel. Only very few did not pass through the tunnel but reached God immediately.

Spirits or souls are able to move very small objects on Earth, very slightly, to convey their messages to those whom they love. It seems that flipping a light switch is comparatively easier for these souls, than to move objects.

Topics of this nature are a 'Taboo' in our society. It is considered evil to talk about spirits. All spirits are called 'evil' spirits. We are so engrossed with our materialistic life that we forget that we are spiritual beings. Even people who have led very pure lives are not believed to have become Angels after their death. This is very unfair. We pray for the departed souls. We can also pray to them for our needs. They will surely heed our call and help us in distress.

How many of us truly believe our religious teachings? Though religion teaches us that we have Angels do we believe it to be true? We think that it is possible only in theory and cannot happen in real life. Media plays a negative role in creating 'devils' and 'vampires' which thrill the audience and fill the box office. Has anybody been beaten up or murdered or swindled by a ghost? No. Only human beings are capable of committing these evils on earth.

Children can see Angels because their minds are not restricted by the taboos of the society. If we can get over our incredulity, and start believing in Angels, they become a part of our lives, as if by magic. They also help us tide over difficult times. A lot of research in Near Death experiences has proved that the people whom we love are with us forever.

We meet them after we die. Life is eternal and our sojourn on Earth is a temporary experience. Life is a test that God gives us. Our performance in this test determines our union with God. I firmly believe that my Angel is with me and will be with me until, and even after I die.

# CHAPTER VIII

## AMMACHI

*Ammachi's* life history is the story of a resilient woman. It is that of a brave woman, who never gave up during adversity. *Ammachi* was fair, graceful and very good looking. In her sixties she looked matronly and still very kind and beautiful, but she had been very good looking when she was young. She was brought up in 'Penang.' Her Father worked for the Postal Department and he had settled at Penang along with his wife and children.

*Ammachi* was every inch the devout Roman Catholic that she was brought up to be, by her parents. Her parents took their little ones to church every day where they had to attend mass. It was a habit practiced by many Christian parents in those days. According to the conventions of those days at least one child in the family joined the religious order, and Ammachi's family was no exception to the rule. Her sister chose to become a Nun in the

'Immaculate Order.' Life was very rosy until tragedy struck the family.

My great grandmother passed away at childbirth and my great grandfather had to take care of the children in an alien land. He also had to look after the new born infant since his wife had passed away. His condition was very pitiable.

His father in law had a proposal to make. He offered to give another one of his daughters in marriage to my great grandfather. He thought that she would be the best person to take care of her sister's family. Nobody else could be expected to look after the children, unless it was one of the siblings of my deceased great grandmother.

*Ammachi's* dad had no other choice and he accepted the proposal. But he had to fulfill a condition. He had to return from Penang to India, because his father in law was not very confident about sending yet another daughter to a foreign country. The whole family returned to India from Penang.

*Ammachi* was only nine years old when the family moved from Penang. She and her siblings continued their education in India and she grew up to be a lovely young woman. She was brought up in a very innocent and religious manner befitting a young woman from a good family. She obeyed her parents unquestioningly. Her stepmother was kind to the children and the family remained united.

When Ammachi was eighteen years old a proposal of marriage was made for her hand. The groom belonged to a family which met the eligibility requirement. Everybody was satisfied.

My grandfather was well educated and he was a *Tahsildar* (a tax collecting officer) in the Government service. This match was thought to be ideal by the parents of the bride and the groom, and the marriage was fixed. In India, an arranged marriage is the only option available to a majority of girls, even these days. *Ammachi* became a bride when she was eighteen. My grandfather was a dark, handsome, and a kind man and life flew on rosy wings.

The only problem was that *Ammachi's* mother- in- law had her own ideas about how a bride in the family should be treated. When *Ammachi* conceived her first child (my mother), her mother- in- law barely gave her enough food to eat, or nutrition to aid the baby's growth, and as a result my mother was very weak at birth. She also had to work throughout the day, to take care of the family.

Probably this was why she had a soft corner for my mother, who passed away before she did. *Ammachi* did not know that very soon her world was going to be shaken thoroughly, and her resilience tested by the challenges of life. My grandfather had intestinal cancer in his late thirties and *Ammachi* was widowed at twenty eight.

My great grandfather was completely devastated upon seeing his daughter widowed at such a young age, and gave her as much support as he could offer. After his death, one of her brothers supported her. *Ammachi* and her four children were supported and guided by her brother, until they were able to manage their family on their own.

An incident which happened in her life proves *Ammachi's* mettle. After being widowed, she attended classes in Tailoring and Arts and Crafts and became an expert in this area. She decided to apply for the post of the Arts and Crafts teacher, in the school where her youngest daughter was studying her tenth grade.

To be eligible for this post, she had to pass her tenth grade examinations. She and her daughter (my aunt) wrote the tenth grade examinations at the same time and *Ammachi* became eligible to teach in the school where her daughter was a student.

It was with great difficulty and perseverance that she managed to find eligible grooms for her three daughters, including my mother. She was blessed with great sons- in -law who cherished her. She also had a very loving daughter in law who treated her like her own mother. All her life was spent on loving and serving others. After she grew old, we noticed some behavioral changes in *Ammachi.* But there was a valid reason.

'I don't know you.' These words were not uttered by a stranger, but by a mother to her children. And these were the words which were uttered by *Ammachi.* She was slowly losing her memory. Her brain could not take the travails of life any longer. She was affected by Dementia. The disease affected her so much that she had forgotten the people who mattered to her the most, in life. But she remembered my maternal uncle, her only son until the last days of her life.

Whenever I visited her, she would smile sweetly with her customary kindness. I would ask her, 'Do you know me *Ammachi?*' I think she must have been embarrassed for not recognizing me, or must have felt sad that she could not remember who I was, though I looked so familiar. She would just ignore the question, without answering me in the negative. *Ammachi* was considerate to the feelings of others until the end of her days, though the effects of her disease were ravaging.

'Why is it imperative to educate the young about the diseases which affect the elderly?' It is important that young people should know the nature of diseases which affect the old. Diseases like 'Parkinson's, Alzheimer's and Dementia induce a lot of behavioral changes. Caretakers are puzzled by such changes and think that their wards exhibit traits of childishness.

They are tempted to judge them for their sudden behavioral changes, without knowing that the reason behind these changes is a diseased brain. That is why we should educate the young, about the nature of such diseases. They will be better equipped to take care of the elders in their families in the future.

When a person we love is treated so unfairly by life, it is natural to ask questions. It is during these times that the mind is perplexed and wonders about the vicissitudes of life. 'Why should people who are so kind and good be treated so unfairly by life?' This was a question I often asked myself when I reflected about my mother and my grandmother and I did not receive the answer to this question, until a spiritual transformation occurred in my own life.

*Ammachi* made exquisite dolls and also dressed them up colorfully. These dolls were adorned with golden colored sequins, which looked very attractive. She had a natural flair for handwork. I thought that she was very ingenious. She also knew crochet and made beautiful sweaters and bags. She tried her best to teach me sewing but I did not have the patience to learn or practice it.

Those were the days when people had never heard of popular brands of chips, and it was the custom of the ladies of the household to prepare mouth-watering snacks and crisps for the members of the household to relish. *Ammachi* attended baking and cooking sessions to learn these skills. I accompanied her to classes where she learnt to prepare fluffy cakes and sweet '*badhushas.* '

I cannot eulogize about her '*adhirasam,*' a delicacy made of rice and jaggery, because it was a failure. The word *adhirasam* literally means 'very tasty' in Tamil. Though it was very tasty, the *adhirasam* which *Ammachi* made, though meant to be soft and succulent was as hard as a rock. We had to break it first before we could eat it, and it lasted for months simply because of the fact that the elders of the household did not have very strong teeth.

I ate the whole lot. I cannot vouch for my brother. The adhirasams became a joke in the family. My *Ammachi* endowed me with her sense of initiative to a major extent. But she never tried to make adhirasams again. I think this was the only effort where she failed to taste success.

The *'Kathiri Veyyil'* season or the peak summer season of May had its own advantages for her simply because she was an expert at making *'Vathal'* or *'Vadaams,'* a South Indian favorite which is very tasty. It is eaten as an accompaniment with rice, crisp and spicy to the right degree. It is a South Indian variation of chips, but a tastier and a healthier version, because it is homemade and has no added preservatives.

Rice is ground coarsely, and cooked in boiling water along with salt, green chilies and cumin seeds. After it is fully cooked and reaches the right consistency it is filled into a '*Murukku Achu*', (a press used to make Murukku, a spicy savory) and pressed through it to make suitable shapes. The shapes could vary according to the *Achu* (press) which is used. Then it is left to dry in the hot Sun until it becomes completely dry. This is deep fried in oil and is very tasty. It can be stored in containers for a long period of time and used when required.

It is also relished as a snack by children. The children of the house had the task of driving away the sparrows and birds which haunted the terraces in which the '*Vathal*' was left to dry in the hot sun. We left black umbrellas to frighten the sparrows and crows, but still some sparrows were daring enough to fly away with a '*Vathal*' or two occasionally, and provoked our ire. We ran after them and shooed them away as best as we could, but since they had the additional advantage of wings we had to accept defeat.

During my Higher Secondary exams, when I was affected by chicken pox *Ammachi* waited outside the exam hall with tender coconut water, worried about my health.

I never thanked my widowed grandmother for all the care that she showered on me. Only after her death did I realize that she was born in the month of August, the same month that I was born in, but I had never celebrated it with her.

I was too young and immature to appreciate her worth. I am sure that she must have understood me and must have forgiven me. When I am faced with difficult circumstances, I reflect about *Ammachi's* will power, and it seems to endow me with strength and passion in my purpose. I have never forgotten her.

Why do some people suffer so much? Would you believe me if I told you that they choose to do so? We make these choices before our birth with the help of our higher spirits or Angels. Research on Near Death experiences has proved this. The survivors say that every soul makes a contract with God. According to this agreement, they are born on earth to face a specific life situation, which has already been determined for them. They also choose to be born to a particular set of parents, for the evolution of their souls on earth.

Every soul in this world has a purpose to achieve, and it is with this intention that it is sent to earth. Souls forget their origins at birth. Gradually they evolve 'consciousness' through their earthly experiences until they become spiritually mature and are ready for their union with God's consciousness.

It is too late in my case to make amends for taking *Ammachi* for granted. It is always possible for the young to be taught to appreciate and love their grand-parents, in the way that they truly deserve to be loved.

Communication has grown so much that it is possible to reach one end of the world from another in a matter of seconds, but the focus of 'Media' and 'Communication' is only on 'Entertainment.' 'Whose fault is it that children grow up without values of empathy and consideration, even towards members of their own families?' Children are brought up amidst 'virtual reality' with no awareness about genuine problems like Global Warming, Violence, or Poverty.

## CHAPTER IX

## COLLEGE DAYS

My College days should have been the most precious days of my life, but I did not understand their value until they ended abruptly, while I was studying the second year of my UG Degree. I gained admission in one of the best Catholic colleges in the city. We had very charming Professors who treated us like grown up women. The women's college was run by the Nuns of the 'Franciscan' order. The staff members were also women.

I was fascinated by the Professors who taught us. One of the Professors addressed us as 'Ladies'. We were never given so much respect at school. I felt it was an honor to be addressed that way. Having just entered College from school, this form of address made us feel important and very happy.

I had to travel by the Public Transport System to College, just as I did to school. The transport system was not very good during those times, and the buses were always crowded during the peak hours. Students from various Schools and Colleges in the city, as well as professionals, used this means of transport as it was economical.

Buses were scarce. We had to be very punctual to board the bus at the right time. If we missed the bus, or if the bus was ahead of its usual schedule for some reason, we would be late to College. Most of the buses never stopped at the bus stands.

Instead, the drivers of the buses would stop them at about fifteen feet away and everybody had to run and board the buses. The people, who ran the fastest, were rewarded with the prize of boarding their buses, and reaching their destinations on time.

It seemed to be such great fun when we were young. But we never considered the difficulties of the senior citizens. My friends who studied in the same College traveled with me, and most of the time we had to travel standing, all the way to our destination.

Now the situation has improved very much and the number of buses has increased to cater to the growing population. The students of the College came dressed in colorful and stylish clothes. We were allowed to wear pants but not allowed to wear 'sleeveless' dresses. The students were disgruntled that such control was exercised by the College, but they had to fall in line with the rules.

Disobedience was not tolerated by the management. My parents were very particular that I should wear traditional clothes. I always wore *half saris* to College. This dress derives its name from the word *sari* which is worn by Indian women. The difference between the two is that the *half saris* are only half the length of saris, and they are draped over full length skirts which touch the feet. Girls who wore *half saris* were 'looked down' upon by these stylish young women.

My craze for reading story books reached gigantic proportions while I was at College, and because I was a teenager I developed a passion for reading romantic novels. I would complete reading at least one book a day. We were not allowed to borrow more than one book a day from the College Library. I would find my favorite books and hide them in another section. The next day, I would pick them up from where I had hidden them the previous day. My brother never read story books. He was always busy with his school books. He was more practical than me.

I had made a wrong choice in neglecting my studies, and I had to bear the consequence of my choice. My father was disappointed with my grades. During my Higher Secondary exams I was down with 'chicken pox' but I managed to score about seventy five percentage overall. My father was very disappointed and chided me for my underperformance.

My brother had a very good academic record and he topped the school results. Because of my aversion towards Mathematics and my passion for reading stories, I was just an average student. I had chosen Economics and Commerce as my Major and Ancillary subjects but found out that I did not like these subjects much. This reflected in my College results, and I just scored average marks in my subjects. I was sorely disappointed with my marks.

My father was extremely critical of my results. He was greatly disappointed and he showed it. He shouted at me. I was very frightened of my father when he got angry. I knew that I had been irresponsible. My parents were justified in their expectations.

I felt miserable for not rising up to the expectations of my parents. I had not been able to identify the right course of study which would have kindled my passion. My parents had given me the freedom to make a choice.

But my negligence was not irreparable. In spite of my playfulness, I was able to make a mark in my profession, later on in life. Every person has a unique role to play, in this world.

Some children are able to identify their goals at an early age, while some take their own time. This flowering of a person's identity should be accepted and encouraged without judgment. I was so upset with my marks that I decided to consent to an early marriage.

The girls from my College belonged to affluent families and they were given a generous amount of pocket money by their parents. But in contrast, my parents were of the opinion that giving money to young people would spoil them. I received a very paltry sum daily as pocket money, but I could not complain.

It was useless to complain. In addition my parents were not rich enough to give money to us, to be wasted on junk food. I do not blame my parents. Most of the Indian parents in the eighties had ideologies which were similar.

All these burdened me with an inferiority complex, as I compared myself with my friends. Those who received a very good daily allowance from their parents weren't even aware of my embarrassment in this regard. But these practices also taught me the value of money and I acquired the habit of never wasting money. Though I was disappointed with not having too much money while growing up, I think it is very good to bring up children that way. Pampering them with too much money is not good for them in the long run.

This habit also helped me to become conscientious about not wasting any kind of resource, including electricity and water. I feel guilty about wasting natural resources even though some resources are freely available. It shocks me to see youngsters as well as the old, wasting natural resources unscrupulously, without thinking about the future generations. Children should be educated about using natural resources conscientiously.

Indiscriminate cutting and burning of trees, unlimited usage of plastic and chemicals, using pesticides without reason, and polluting our water sources, is damaging our bonding with the Universal consciousness. Rising above these practices enables one to create a spiritual bonding with God himself. If we accept him as our Creator, we should know that destroying his Creation would sadden him.

The attitude of carelessness towards using our resources is costing us heavily. Global warming has become a major threat to our planet. Youngsters have begun questioning the leaders of the world for ignoring 'climate change' which is wreaking havoc

everywhere.

# CHAPTER X

## A ROYAL PERSONAGE

My mother- in- law was a source of inspiration to me. She was one of the most dignified human beings that I have ever met. My perception about her has changed a lot now, from the time since I met her first. She was almost sixty years old during my wedding, and I had just turned eighteen. My mother in law bore eight children and raised them up in a very affectionate and secure manner.

I have always witnessed joy in her household and she was the 'Royal queen.' My Father- in- law was an esteemed judge and was a very pious man. My mother- in- law was responsible for taking care of the children and the household.

After my wedding, I was unsure of the role that I had to play in the kitchen and my mother in law's expectations from me, and I felt uncomfortable. I was filled with dread whenever I entered her kitchen. This fear continued for a long time. The kitchen was my mother- in -law's fortress, where she reigned supreme. She never uttered a harsh word to me but my sense of inadequacy made me feel insecure. I had already judged myself as incapable of meeting her expectations.

The shelves of the kitchen were always immaculate and shining; pots and pans were arranged meticulously in the places allotted to them. The utensils that were used for cooking every day were cleaned by the maid, and spread out on the cemented floor to dry under sunlight. The sprawling house of nearly eight thousand square feet was managed very efficiently by her.

Because of my in- expertise in cooking, I mostly stayed away from the kitchen. But I would volunteer to cut the vegetables, like a devotee intent on pleasing the deity. She must have smiled at my ignorance but I never heard a word of reproach from her. I learned to dice vegetables in a very fine manner, from one of the household help. We would sit together to cut the vegetables for the day. My mother -in- law never asked me to assist in the kitchen, and I took the situation for granted. She never spoke much, but was the most patient woman that I have ever met.

One of the most important things that I admired about her was her slender fingers. The reason was that these fingers were skilled in preparing intricate delicacies which were perfect in taste and flavor. The *Gulab Jamuns* (a very tasty milk sweet) that she made were perfect, and just melted in the mouth like butter. They were oval and identical in their shapes and they were the best that you could ask for. They were even better than the ones available in the best sweet shops.

The mutton cutlets that she made were perfect in shape and flavor. I have never seen any one of her dishes go awry. The meticulous attention given to details always fascinated me. She would first cook the minced mutton and prepare the gravy with onions and tomatoes. Then she would mash the potatoes with her slender fingers delicately until the mixture was completely soft. She would then apply oil to the palm of her hands, and shape every cutlet superbly. I would watch her hands perform the task diligently, and wonder how the dishes that I cooked always tasted different every time.

Thereafter, the cutlets would be fried until they reached a golden brown color and placed on a platter. Every cutlet would look superb and tempting to the eye. The whole household was mesmerized with her cooking skills. In fact every single dish that she cooked was her 'signature dish' and her family was very blessed.

My husband loved her very much and passed witty remarks to make her smile. Every time that he went out on business, she would wait until he returned, to eat lunch with him. She was a very pious woman and entrusted her life to God's will. She was a devout Catholic throughout her life.

I have never seen her miss the Mass even a single day in her life. Towards the end of her days, when she was completely confined to the bed, she was unable to go to church. She would watch the Mass on television. She never watched serials on the television. This was not because she did not have the time, but because she was not interested. She was always engaged in taking care of household matters and she was busy until eleven p.m. every night.

The mind creates its own fantasies. My mother- in- law's perfection made me anxious and I became afraid of not measuring up to her expectations. This pressure was building up in my heart. It was ready to burst at the slightest excuse. I was too young to realize her magnanimity.

One day I rebelled against her, without any valid reason. But she forgave me completely and my love for her was established forever. She never discussed the matter after that and loved me as unconditionally as she had done earlier.

There is a practice among Christian families where the young go down on their knees, to get the blessings of the elders in the family. Every single time that I knelt down on my knees to seek her blessing after that incident was to seek forgiveness from her. I did not do it explicitly but kept it within my heart.

I think she must have felt it too. Just like in my mother's case, I was not able to take care of my mother- in- law when she was on her death bed. But she was taken care of very well, by her children living in the same city.

Her eyes always emitted kindness. They changed color after she grew old, and turned to a slight shade of grey. They seemed to be full of compassion and I felt forgiven and loved. Just like my parents and *Ammachi,* she epitomized the virtue of sacrifice.

Her life was an example of how to completely remain detached from the 'Ego' and its expectations. She performed acts of love and service without expecting reward or praise.

Today, I realize that we need not do anything extraordinary to touch other people's lives. Doing what we can with complete commitment and love is what life is all about. Achievements are temporary. They may change with time. But what remains forever is the impact we make in people's hearts.

## CHAPTER XI

## GOD WITH US

Meanwhile I was truly happy to teach young children and was very passionate about my job. I had enough fluency and knowledge to teach them, but I still did not possess a degree in Education. The Principal who had offered me the post made it very clear, that I would lose my job if I did not complete my Bachelor's Training in Education. But this was almost impossible, as there was no institution in the vicinity offering this course, and I could never leave my children to complete this training elsewhere.

I spent sleepless nights wondering about how I would be affected if I lost my job. I had begun loving my job too much and the thought of losing it disturbed me. I did not work for the salary. The salary was a pittance, and since my husband was employed well we did not need the money. But I would lose my purpose in life.

A priest in the college where my husband worked was interested in helping students who had dropped out from school and college. He had founded an organization to help the poor children of the town where we lived. He was supported by the philanthropists in the area. The organization still exists at 'Tirupattur,' the town where we lived for the most part of our lives.

He offered computer education to the underprivileged, the ordinary workers and *coolies* (daily wage earners). He also provided a program for drop-outs from the University. It was an Open University Program from 'IGNOU' (Indira Gandhi National Open University). This University was affiliated to the College, and the Professors from the College would teach the learners during the weekend. During the year that I faced the threat of losing my job, the University offered a course in Teachers Training which was recognized by the Government. It was a striking *synchronicity* which was of immense use to me, and a boon to the small town.

The only difficulty was that the University had high standards and it conducted an Entrance Examination to admit students to the course. There were very few seats, and I was not sure that I could manage to get admitted to the Program.

I appeared for the examination, and luckily all the books that I had read throughout my life, helped me to pass my Entrance Examination. I secured the seventeenth rank in the nation. The Examination did not test memory skills but it tested Language, Vocabulary, and Grammar skills.

I found it very advantageous. I was the only person to pass this entrance Examination from my town that year. The 'course' was withdrawn from my town from the next year onwards. But I remain eternally grateful to the Priest, Rev. Father Thomas, who made it possible for me to complete my degree in Education.

My husband helped me and supported my zeal for completing my Education. I taught at school during the day and studied in the evenings. I also taught my children who were very young, regularly in the evenings. I still wonder about how my life would have changed if this *synchronicity* had not occurred. At this stage of my life, I have realized, that nothing happens by chance or coincidence, and everything happens for a reason.

The passion that a person has for something goes a long way, in helping to make a dream come true. Enabling me to complete my degree was God's gift to me. I also believe that it was a gift from my deceased mother who knew how much I had yearned for completing my Degree.

I continued teaching in the same school for ten years. Many teachers, who were my colleagues left for the Government service since it was very lucrative, but I never tried for a position in a Government School because money has never been the greatest priority in life. I was also endowed with enough financial security to lead a comfortable life.

I enjoyed working in the school, because it seemed like a continuation of my school days. My Education had also been completed in a school belonging to the same religious order for which I worked, and I felt at ease in this setting.

Life went on as usual until tragedy struck us. My husband noticed something unusual about his health. He was detected with cancer in the year 1997. The prognosis was confirmed by a very close family friend of my brother in law. The doctors expected the worst because he had ignored the symptoms for almost a year. They advised him to get the operation done immediately.

Fortunately he was operated by experts and he was cured. Again, it was a miracle as the cancer had not spread at all, though the symptoms had existed for almost a year. Since he was only forty at that time, the doctors were in a quandary about whether he should receive 'Chemotherapy.' Almost all the other doctors in the team recommended Chemotherapy except one. Her name was 'Faith.' She was very certain that the therapy would be very harmful to my husband. She felt that he did not require it. After much discussion, the other doctors too agreed with her opinion. My husband was very much relieved because we knew that Chemotherapy was a difficult procedure. We were thankful to God for his great mercy.

After this incident, one of my colleagues compelled me to accompany her to an astrologer. She had a lot of marital problems and wanted to find a solution. I was very reluctant because I had no belief in astrology, and thought that all astrologers were fake people. Besides, my religious beliefs proclaimed very strongly against this practice. But I accompanied her because I felt sorry for her.

The astrologer was a simple man and I don't recollect anything special about his appearance. But what he told me was quite interesting, though it was too difficult for me to believe. I never believed that spirits could communicate with humans, and thought that astrological predictions were just a ploy for making money.

To my incredulity, the astrologer told me, that a deceased female ancestor from my family had saved my husband's life. This ancestor did not want to see me suffer at a very young age. I was not fully convinced by his revelations during that time.

After having witnessed many *miracles* and *synchronicities*, I think that it must be true. This does not in any way undermine the faith that I have for the doctors who treated my husband, but there are crucial issues like the detection of the disease, which play a major role in cure.

It was the power of the Almighty, which revealed his cancer before it had progressed beyond cure. A question that I asked myself was, 'Why isn't everybody cured in this miraculous manner?' Near Death survivors reveal that nobody can reach the gates of Heaven before their duly appointed time. That is why these survivors are sent back to Earth. They also receive the communication that they cannot remain in Heaven, because their purpose in life has not yet been fulfilled.

I thank God for having protected my husband so that he could continue his profession without any challenges, until his retirement. I now know that nothing happens through coincidence, and that God endowed him with a second chance to live. According to Near Death survivors, prayers help to raise positive vibrations. The prayers offered by my mother in law must have also aided his cure. I also believe in the astrologer's statement that a deceased ancestor (my mother) had been my Angel and my advocate to God.

There was another incident which made us feel the protection of our Angels in a very dramatic manner. We were driving to Madras and had travelled more than half the distance. My husband was driving at about forty kilometers an hour because there was heavy traffic on either side of us.

We saw a number of Container Trucks carrying goods on either sides of our vehicle. Before we could realize it, the Truck on the right hit our car and started dragging it. It was a very frightening experience to be tossed about in the car. It lasted only a few minutes. I was completely dazed and did not realize what was happening to us.

Our car was pushed to the middle of the road and it hit the median and stopped. Luckily the driver of the Truck had applied his brakes and brought it under control. I turned to look at my husband and was happy that he was unharmed.

Neither of us had even a scratch on our bodies. It was truly a 'miracle.' All the vehicles on the road had stopped and people surrounded the car to see what had happened to us. They were happy to see us unharmed. Though the car was damaged, we were able to drive it the rest of the distance to our destination. We marveled and thanked God for his kindness.

# CHAPTER XII

## MY FATHER AND ME

Every person's relationship with a parent is unique and I am not an exception. The feelings that my father evoked in me were a mixture of awe, admiration and fear. He was a perfectionist. I think that he was an awesome dad because his qualities were unique. He was a strict 'disciplinarian' throughout his life, and was completely honest in his dealings. He expected the same from everybody. My parents were well adjusted, as my mother must have realized that whatever my father decided was always in the best interests of the family.

My father worked for the 'Secretariat' in Madras city. He would leave at around eight in the mornings as he had a long commute and was always punctual to work. He would cycle all the way to the Railway station and park his cycle in the parking area. Then he would board an electric train to the 'Fort Station.' The Station acquired its name from the Fort which was built during the British rule in India. The fort was called Fort. St. George after the patron Saint of England St. George, as it was completed on 23$^{rd}$ April, 1644, which was his feast day.

It was built by the East India Company for the purpose of promoting trade. Since the time the British left, the local Government functions in this Fort. It is a very beautiful edifice and looks very inspiring. I thought that my father was a great person to work for the Government.

I was fully justified in feeling proud about him because even though he worked during a period when corruption was rampant my father did not receive bribes. He lived a very authentic life. He often lamented against the political decisions made by the parties in power, which were sometimes detrimental to the welfare of the State, and only beneficial to the ruling party.

My father always helped my mother to pack our lunches to school. He would spread a generous helping of butter and jam on slices of bread in the morning for breakfast. We would find an equal number of bread slices spread with butter and jam. We loved *Modern bread.* This bread is made by the Modern Bread Company which makes delicious bread.

Sometimes we had *fruit bread,* which was a treat. Frequently my mother prepared *idlis* (steamed round shaped eatables made of rice and black gram) with spicy *chutneys* (dips). Boiled eggs were an essential part of our lunches because they were easy to cook and we loved them.

My father helped my mother in setting up the table for breakfast. Sometimes he scraped coconuts for her. Coconuts were always included in our meals in one form or another. They were either scraped to garnish vegetables, or ground and used for preparing curries. My father used to sit on a chair before the dining table and perform this task diligently. He helped my mother finish her cooking on time.

Today, I appreciate the fact that my father did not consider it beneath his dignity to assist my mother in cooking. It showed his love for the family. He was almost a trendsetter because many men still believe that cooking or helping in the kitchen is beneath a man's dignity. My parents never solicited my help in this regard. I regret that I was insensitive to my mother's hard work. I wish I had helped her more and shared her burden.

Probably this was an ideology promoted on the basis of sacrifice. Parents believe that they have to sacrifice everything for their children. It would be better for parents to discuss their expectations from their children in a healthy manner. They could take their children into confidence, instead of burdening themselves. Children can also benefit from their sharing as they will understand life better.

Since I was not very much pampered with gifts while I grew up, I remember the first gift which my father bought for me. It was a beautiful watch with a gold colored dial and a brown leather strap. I still preserve the watch. I must have been twelve or thirteen when I received this gift.

Probably I had asked for a watch. I do not remember. But I did not expect it to be so beautiful. My father must have thought that I deserved it. My parents did not lavish us with gifts very often.

My brother was deprived of these small joys of life, because my mother was already sinking when he joined College. We were knee deep in financial trouble.

Gifts become more precious when they are given with a reason, and when they are not given too often. Too many gifts, given without reason may not be fully appreciated in the long run, as children may assume that it is a 'parental duty' to give gifts, and even take them for granted.

Another gift that my parents brought me was a beautiful ornate gold necklace with a pendant. It was customary for brides to be given gold ornaments during their weddings and all Indian parents shoulder the responsibility of accumulating gold jewels for their daughters, almost as soon as they are born. In spite of the fact that these days, some grooms do not demand anything, it is almost considered as a moral responsibility of the parents to give gifts of gold to the bride.

The necklace was a huge one and it had designs of flowers which were linked to one another. It also had a set of matching earrings. My parents never believed in buying jewels embedded with precious stones as they thought that these jewels did not have any resale value. But I liked jewels which were studded with precious stones, as the sparkling colored stones caught my attention, and looked very attractive to the eye.

Though my parents understood my disappointment, their resolve against buying jewels embedded with stones remained firm and they did not relent. Later, I was very happy and grateful to receive a set of 'diamond earrings' as a gift from my mother in law. This set of earrings sparkled brightly and satisfied my cravings. It was adequate compensation for not possessing jewels embedded with precious stones.

After a few years, I exchanged the ornate necklace for another necklace which was lighter and more intricately designed, but I lost some money in the exchange. I have the huge earrings with the flower design, which still look new because I have not worn them too often.

I felt guilty that I was not able to like the necklace, which was a loving gift from my parents. It was bought with their hard earned money. But I was not able to compromise my liking for their happiness. It is important that parents should consider the wishes of their children, when making decisions that would have a major impact on their lives.

When the children are given the right to make a choice, they become responsible for the consequences which arise from that choice. Parents also need not regret the choices that the children make for themselves as they have every right to do so. Each and every choice, results in a certain pattern of consequences, which is essential for the evolution of every soul in the Universe.

My father had to come to terms with the fact, that his wife would leave her earthly abode just when he retired from service. Being the hard working couple that they were, my parents had never really enjoyed their lives but had always sacrificed their needs for their children. They had made some simple plans of travelling after my father's retirement.

My father was never able to reconcile with the fact that he could not fulfill his wife's longing for travel. These regrets caused him a lot of suffering. Probably he had to endure this pain for his soul's evolution. But I never noticed a flaw in either of my parents as long as they lived. They were a perfect couple.

After my mother's death my father lived partly in Chennai (with my brother) and partly with me, in the town where I lived. I consider it my greatest blessing that my husband was very affectionate towards my father and had the greatest respect for him.

Until my wedding, my father's word was law to me and I never argued with him. After my wedding I was considered mature enough to make my own decisions. I was upset with my father for having been too strict with me. I started wearing fashionable clothes which I was not allowed to wear before my wedding. But these were negligible facts, and my love for my father never diminished, as I knew that he always did what he thought was best for me.

My father never missed physical exercise, but suffered from heart ailment after my mother passed away. He was a good 'gymnast' when he was at school and received a lot of prizes and certificates. He was also a very good singer and had a melodious voice. He had developed his musical aptitude while he studied at 'St. Joseph's College, Tiruchy.'

When he was in his sixties, he developed symptoms of Parkinson's which had a debilitating effect on him. His illness affected me badly, because I found it very difficult come to terms with the fact that my 'hero' of the yesteryears had become very weak and frail, and had to rely on me for support.

God sent us help even in the worst of circumstances, and our household help whom we affectionately addressed as 'watchman' gave him company and solace when he was sick. In addition, towards the end of his life he enjoyed the company of my granddaughter who was one year old. This period was very trying, but also as the most wonderful period of my whole life.

Though it was painful to see my father getting worse, I had the gratification of serving him.

Parkinson's is a deadly disease and it affects the patient like slow poison. As the disease progresses, the patient's face becomes masked and becomes devoid of expression. Taking care of patients suffering from chronic illnesses requires patience and affection. I do not claim to have been a perfect caretaker. Sometimes, I would become upset when my dad behaved unreasonably, but I kept myself updated with information so that I could be aware of the nature of his disease.

I realized that it was not my father's fault, but the disease that was at fault for his paranoid behavior. I would inform our house hold help that his sudden mood swings were caused by his disease and it was not his original nature to behave the way he did.

My father was always affectionate towards the people who assisted us. He would give them gifts that they could use regularly, like blankets or dresses. He would buy them rice and groceries on special occasions. I was blessed with the most wonderful parents that anyone could ask for.

## CHAPTER XIII

## CLAIRAUDIENCE

I was brought up in such a protected environment that sometimes I shied away from seeing visitors who visited us at home, especially if they were young and belonged to the opposite sex. This was considered normal in the eighties when I was a teenager. I was also afraid of the dark, and the ghosts which were thought to be lurking in the dark .These ghosts seemed to exist with the sole purpose of possessing human beings, according to popular literature and media.

When I was almost twelve years old, I heard of a neighbor being possessed by an evil spirit. A priest was called to drive away the spirit which had possessed her. After these developments, I never ventured down the stairs after six in the evening, because of the fear of getting possessed. The 'possession' became a favorite topic in the street. I was especially afraid of walking down the stairs because I could see the neighbor's window which was always open, and sometimes I could catch a glimpse of her sitting on the chair. I would dash down the stairs, not caring if I fell down and hurt myself in the bargain.

This fear reached such gigantic proportions that I would lie down at night and think of the imaginary spirits waiting to frighten me. To this day I am afraid of the dark, especially when I am alone.

After my mother passed away the house became desolate, and all the warmth of the house disappeared with her. But I was a regular visitor to Madras. When I started pursuing my 'Doctorate' I had to go to my hometown to visit the library. I loved to visit Madras as it had a special place in my heart.

Sometimes I traveled with my father. Often I traveled alone, and complete my work in a day or two and return home. On one of my regular visits to my house, I felt very unhappy and was obsessed with the thoughts of my mother. I felt grief pervading every single cell of my body. I had missed her very badly after giving birth to my son.

She could not visit me after my son's birth because she was very ill. I had to take him to the hospital, where she was admitted, almost immediately after he was born, because my mother was frantic to see him. She was critically ill and had no energy to speak but she remarked, 'He looks as tender as a rose.'

After my mother's death I placed a small photograph of my mother where I could see it regularly, and I prayed to her. This became a regular habit with me and I realized that my prayers were being granted. I never spoke about my mother very often because it kindled the grief which was deeply buried within the recesses of my heart.

This was the same emotion that was predominant in me that evening. I was dusting the table. The table was long and it was made of teak wood. It had six chairs. My father always made sure that everything that he bought was of good quality. Though we could not afford luxury, the house looked neat and simple.

It pained me to see that a lot of dust had accumulated over the surface of the table. This was because we visited Madras only once in a few months. The memories of childhood came flooding back in all its innocence. I was fully engrossed in my thoughts when I heard a noise very close to my ears. It was a human voice but it did not make any sense.

I was startled out of my wits, and all the fear that was buried in me all along, resurfaced. I returned back to the town where I lived, the next day but it took some time for me to get over my fear completely. I consoled myself with the thought that I must have imagined the sound.

Nothing happened for a very long time. Life went on as usual. Time passed but the thoughts of my mother never diminished from my heart. One day I was in the kitchen, and fully engrossed with preparations for cooking. The washed utensils lay neatly stacked on a counter. Suddenly, one vessel moved very slightly making a distinct noise.

Nobody except me was in the kitchen. There was no possibility for the vessel to move from its place. I was shocked. These incidents happened occasionally and without any particular reason. The sounds made by spirits are barely audible and can be heard only in complete silence. I would hear the door being closed slightly when there was nobody around. But this was done in a very discreet manner and was not at all frightening.

I never shared these experiences with anybody, because all these topics are considered to be 'taboo' in society. We prefer to watch horror movies and be scandalized by the gory details that these movies portray.

Man has completely buried himself in the material aspects of the world, that even God's endeavors to reach him are being met with disbelief. It is more convenient to deny these aspects, as we don't have time for them.

We attribute these kinds of supernatural events to evil spirits but in my experience I have felt the reassuring presence of my Angel.

Often, a door which had been locked at night would mysteriously become unlocked, while we were sleeping. This happened with one particular door all the time. I grew used to these proceedings without becoming anxious.

I also realized that I was able to find articles, which were considered to be lost and forgotten, for quite some time. My cousin missed her gold necklace for quite some time. She was very close to me and I felt sorry for her loss. She had kept it in the locker in her house. It had vanished forever! She had checked the locker many times but it was missing.

She told me this when I visited her house. We were standing before her Almirah discussing her loss. Without a second thought, I put my hand inside the locker spontaneously, and groped for the necklace. Lo and behold! The necklace was dangling in my hands. Another incident of a similar nature also occurred in her house. Probably our energies matched very well and worked for us in our favor. She had missed one of her daughter's earrings for over two months. She had lost any hope of finding it after searching for it everywhere.

She mentioned this to me when I visited her house. The maid was sweeping the floors of the house, as we were speaking. There was a table in the kitchen and I spontaneously instructed the maid to sweep around the legs of the table.

As if by miracle the 'earring' came out of its hiding place and sparkled in the dust. The maid who had swept it out of its hiding place did not notice it, but I did. Like anybody else I thought that these were coincidences. But later I realized that they were not merely coincidental. Rather than considering these incidents as accidental, I realized that they were drawing my attention to something spiritual, and I thanked God for my experiences.

In fact I once remarked to a friend, while narrating about these incidents that I was more afraid of thieves and murderers, rather than these harmless elements which threatened human imagination. I find it difficult to believe that I have overcome the fear of spirits which had threatened me very greatly, when I was

young. I have still not overcome my fear of the dark.

# CHAPTER XIV

## PRAYER AND CONSCIOUSNESS

The experiences recounted by many of the Near Death survivors, lay emphasis on Prayer. Many of them have revealed that chanting of prayers enhances the field of vibration, which is required to reach God. God accepts all our prayers without prejudice, because they are the pleas of the battered souls to the divine. The saying that Faith can move mountains is not false.

My parents made sure that we recited our daily prayers. As children we always recited the 'family prayer' on our knees. Every evening before dinner, my mother would call us to pray. We would kneel down before the picture of 'Jesus Christ' and recite our prayers. There was a list of prayers specifically created to suit a variety of circumstances. Some of these prayers had a lot of intentions covered, and were like an 'insurance' against many of the ills which struck mankind. These prayers had been handed down over the generations and were very special.

My favorite prayer was the one to my Angel, because for me my Guardian Angel was my Knight in shining armor. The Prayer is as follows;

> Angel of god, my Guardian dear,
>
> To whom his love entrusts me here,
>
> Ever this day, be at my side,
>
> To Light and guard,
>
> To rule and Guide,
>
> Amen

When my granddaughter was old enough to speak, I taught her this prayer and she immediately added to it saying, 'Ever this day and night, be at both my sides.' This improvisation had never occurred to me, even though I had been reciting it for many years. I realized that she believed firmly in her Angel. That is why she was able to say it convincingly. Such is the faith of children, which can move mountains. As we grow older, we stop believing in miracles, and so they stop happening for us.

For many, prayers are endless lists of petitions. It is not wrong to implore for God's mercy, but prayers which just focus on 'materialism' are too self centered. A prayer should always be a submission of our will towards God's will. It should be a complete surrender of our intentions, with the faith that everything will happen at the time chosen by God.

It does not mean that we should give up our own efforts, when we pray. Rather, we should pray with the belief that our prayers will be answered at God's chosen time.

There is something about the human 'Ego' which comes Prayer's way. Even though we pray to God to fulfill our intentions, we secretly believe that it is our own effort that has borne fruit. So after a prayer is answered, we forget to be grateful. We start praying for the next intention on the priority list.

The role of 'gratitude' in prayer cannot be neglected. A prayer of 'gratitude' is a soul's song of thankfulness to God. It raises man's consciousness and becomes the doorway to enter God's kingdom.

When I was very young I prayed very fervently for my mother who had conceived. The doctor proclaimed that she was very weak, and there was a solemn air around the house. I was aware that something was amiss and full of fear that my mother would die. Sometimes a prayer arises out of fear for the well being of those who are the closest to us. This baby which was about to arrive, was the fourth in the family. My mother had already given birth to a still born baby boy before I was born.

The baby was born but she suffered from Septicemia, and her blood turned septic. She died when she was just twenty one days old and suffered a lot when she was alive. It was an instance where our prayers were not granted. We were filled with sorrow. God must have had his reasons for taking away the innocent soul.

Reciting prayers, without practicing love for other human beings is a waste of time. God can never be hoodwinked in this manner. We begin doubting God when our prayers are not answered. We set a time limit for God to answer our prayers, according to our limited perceptions.

God answers everybody's prayers. We believe that God turns away from the sinner, but the Bible proclaims that God loves the sinner. The parables of 'The lost Sheep' and 'The Prodigal Son,' narrate how God chooses to go in search of those who have forgotten him. This search is definitely not to find the sinner and punish him but to bring him into God's infinite love.

The Biblical words ring true in this regard, "Which of you men, if you had one hundred sheep, and lost one of them, wouldn't leave the ninety-nine in the wilderness, and go after the one that was lost, until he found it? When he has found it, he carries it on his shoulders, rejoicing.

Nobody is excluded from 'God's love. God's love is so unconditional that he does not shun even the unworthy. When we desire to change for the better, he and his Angels are there to guide us. Though we may have a long way to go to reach perfection, we could always take the first step.

There are instances of miraculous healings happening all over the world, which cannot be explained by Science. These healings happen during prayer. These cannot be dismissed as inconsequential. Near Death Experiences are also parts of God's plan. God makes no mistakes or oversights.

Many such incidents which have been occurring recently prove that new messengers are being sent to instruct mankind. They carry the message that there is a realm beyond that of human understanding and research, and it is the eternal realm. These messengers restore our faith in God and Prayer.

## CHAPTER XV

## MONEY AND CAREER DECISIONS

I was fiercely protective about my children. I rode a 'moped' which I used to drop them at school, and bring them back home, when they were young. I was never late to drop or pick them up from school. I made sure that they participated in programs and competitions organized at school. My world revolved around them.

My daughter showed traces of independence at a very early age. Besides her regular schooling, I taught her additionally at home until she completed her fifth grade. By the time she was in the sixth grade, she was completely independent. Her school was quite close to our house. She did not have to travel on the highway to reach her school.

It was time for my son to go to High School. The only boys' school which offered wholesome education was the one where I started working later. But my son had to travel on the Highway to reach the school. Drivers drove the buses very rashly along these roads, and there was no effective system in place to control them. Accidents and loss of lives are very common in the area.

One of the students from the School where I worked lost his life, in an accident on the Highway. Thinking about this gave me nightmares as I was afraid to let my son travel alone, after so many years of dropping him personally at school.

This was also one of the reasons why I decided to apply for a position in the school where my son was about to be admitted. We would set off to the school together and come back together in the evenings. After a few years my son started going to school on his bicycle, along with his friends. He too preferred to be on his own rather than cling to me for support. It was good that he became independent.

The school encouraged   altruistic tendencies and because it was a Catholic School and was run by Priests, there were regular masses everyday for the residential students and for the Catholics who lived nearby. 'Holy Mass' was arranged on the First Friday of every month in which all the Catholic students took part.

The school also conducted special tuition classes for poor students belonging to the local community, every evening. Small articles of daily use were collected from the wealthy students and offered during the Mass, during the offertory procession. I was greatly interested in encouraging the young students, to share what they could with their less fortunate brethren.

Students belonging to other religions never had prejudices against visiting the chapel. Nobody was forced to come to the chapel, but they were also not prohibited from doing so. Many would visit the chapel especially on the days examinations were held, to make sure that they did well in their exams. It may sound ludicrous but probably this practice fostered courage to help them face something that they were afraid of.

On the first Friday of every month bars of bathing soaps, toothpaste, pencils and note books would be collected and offered during the Mass. Students always responded very enthusiastically to my exhortations to be generous. I used these opportunities to emphasize upon the importance of 'gratitude.' I always spoke to the students about the importance of being grateful to one's parents.

Parents should inculcate the quality of 'gratitude' among their children. This quality cannot appear all of a sudden, unless it is cultivated with care in the early years. It is also beneficial to parents in the long run, as children would be supportive of them when they become old.

Feeling grateful for what we receive, is a vital ingredient for the growth of a soul. A soul which always wants more and more without being grateful can never feel fulfilled, irrespective of the circumstances. The activities fostered in the school gave me a lot of satisfaction.

Another important event that I looked forward to every year was the Sports Day. It was always celebrated in a very grand manner in the school and 'practice' would start almost before a month. The Sports Master would assume an air of importance as he would play a decisive role in the Sports Events. The list of responsibilities would be printed and displayed on the notice boards, for the students as well as the teachers.

As soon as the list was pinned to the notice board, the students flocked around it to know the list of events. The teachers were also equally curious to know their responsibilities, for it entailed a lot of work.

The Sports Master had a lot of responsibilities when the school commenced every academic year. At the beginning of every year, students belonging to every class were distributed equally by the Sports Master among four houses. These houses were named after four Saints, namely, Bosco, Rua, Savio and Thomas.

Each house had a teacher in charge, and the other teachers played the roles of assistants. Students had their own favorites among the teachers. These were the teachers who motivated them well and spared no effort to make their House win the 'Rolling Trophy' for the year.

Making 'House Tents,' was always an area which needed a lot of work, both from the students as well as the teachers. Students would compete with each other in contributing ideas and decorative material. Planning for the Sports day would be done in a very secretive manner. Spies would be appointed in every House to collect ideas. This was done by the students to make sure that their House performed better than the others.

On the Sports day, the entrances to the tents were decorated with brightly colored 'Rangoli' designs. The House which constructed the best tent bagged a Special Prize. It was truly a wonderful celebration. There were prizes for cheering, tent making, discipline and many other skills. The main focus would lie on the events which usually progressed over the week to culminate on the Sports Day.

The House which won the 'Trophy' had a wonderful celebration immediately after the events were over. Drums were beaten, and leaders carried around the playground by the students belonging to the 'winning' House to celebrate their success.

Since I was an English teacher I was given the opportunity of making announcements and the general Commentary, throughout the Sports Day. Usually there was a requirement for two Commentators to coordinate the events. I would prepare my Commentary the previous day itself, with highlights of Sports Events from International Sports, which had made a mark in the minds of the public recently.

School authorities from the neighboring schools and all the parents were invited to the event. It was a 'gala' function and I thoroughly enjoyed being a part of the proceedings. The Closing Ceremony, when the Sports flag was brought down to be kept safe for the next Sports Day, was a solemn event, and I loved it just as much as every student of the school.

It is said that if you love your profession, work becomes joy and this was my sentiment during the years of my teaching career. Focusing primarily on money rewards would have made my life miserable. So why did I leave the school which I loved so much?

I left school to teach in the local College after I realized that my health would be affected, if I continued working until retirement. It had also been my dream to teach Literature, to college students and my dream was fulfilled. My mother's health problems had taught me the value of taking care of my health. I was paid lesser when I became an Assistant Professor than what I was paid to be a school teacher. I did not mind at all. I also realized that I would not feel fulfilled if I remained a teacher at school.

Preoccupations with money make a person mechanical, and forego the simple pleasures that life has to offer. On the contrary when we enjoy our profession, every memorable incident stays with us forever.

It is true that money is essential for meeting the daily needs of life. I usually saved my salary for some months and made small investments in buying jewels.

Time passed quickly and it was time for my son to leave school and join College. He left us to join a University which was quite far away from our town.

My children are deeply religious and I am very proud of them. The following words of 'Kahlil Gibran' always cross my mind when I miss my children, 'Your children are not your children. They are the sons and daughters of Life's longing for itself. They come through you but not from you, and though they are with you yet they belong not to you.' This offers me a lot of solace when I miss them very badly.

My son's education passed uneventfully and very soon he had finished his Professional course and was placed in a good company. But it was a challenging period, because there was a serious economic recession in the US, and as a result there was an unfavorable impact in all the countries of the world.

He had to wait for his 'appointment order' for almost a year. I was very worried for his sake because it was a very difficult period for him. He worked for a company which required him to work nightshifts. To his credit, his religious leanings and his very strong convictions carried him through these difficult times. His patience and prayers were rewarded.

Religion provides us with hope and determination and courage, in times of adversity, if it becomes a way of life. While he was waiting for his appointment order, we undertook a travel to Chennai, for a short spell. After completing our work we were returning back home. It took us almost four hours of travel by train to reach Tirupattur, where we lived, and we always came very early to the 'Central Station' as we were afraid of missing our train.

As usual we came early, and the train was due to arrive in an hour's time. I told my son that he could check his mails if he wanted while waiting for the train and he left to the 'Internet Cafe.' He looked excited when he came back after some time. He told me that he had received his appointment order through mail, and he had to join his office the next morning at Poona. To reach

Poona from Madras, one had to travel for almost twenty hours by train.

It was impossible to reach his destination the next morning, unless he boarded a flight. We went to Tirupattur according to our plan since he had to submit his certificates at the office. The certificates were at home.

The next morning he returned to Madras and boarded a flight, to join work. The mail was his final reminder to report to the office and we failed to receive any other mode of communication. Probably it had been lost in transit.

This incident was too striking to be a mere coincidence. If my son had not checked his mail that evening, things would have changed entirely. Many incidents in our lives are considered to be coincidental in nature. But when these coincidences become habitual and make a pattern, they assume a spiritual nature, and become *synchronicities*. I was always grateful for what I received and acknowledged it constantly.

## CHAPTER XVI

## IMPORTANCE OF THE DIVINE WILL

What is Divine Will? It means that God's plans are different from ours. Our plan has to be approved by God. Without his approval we cannot accomplish our plans. We need a lot of maturity to understand that everything may not happen exactly as we plan.

It does not mean that we should stop planning, or that we should be pessimistic in our expectations. It means that we should be prepared to wait, sometimes even for years, for our plans to bear fruition. After making an effort we should entrust the results into God's hands.

We cannot underestimate a human being's role in any undertaking, but there are thousands of forces which come into play for any effort to bear fruit. It is important for the Ego to acknowledge God's role in any happening. Sometimes when our plans get delayed, we make hasty decisions. It happens because our Ego is not able to accept defeat. This false pride based on the Ego, can sometimes be associated with the family mindset in which a child has been raised. It could arise out of some lack of attention in childhood, when a child is sidelined in favor of the more successful ones.

When the child grows up this is manifested under different circumstances, and reaches a point of becoming quite uncomfortable for the individual and for those around him. I was fortunate to have parents who never compared my academic credentials with my brother's. They never compared my grades with my brother's and I never felt a lack. There was no need for me to resort to my egoistic impulses.

Relationships also become sour when they are poisoned by the Ego. An easy way to overcome our egoistic impulses is to realize that there are no 'separations,' among mankind. All differences are man- made and specially devised to control others. Everybody is equal irrespective of Religion, Status, Gender, Caste or Color. The Ego finds a way to try to assert its superiority, if it believes that it is better than the others in one of the above mentioned list.

Marital problems occur because one of the partners is firmly entrenched in such views of difference. If a man is raised to believe that he is superior to his wife, he will not give her the freedom that she deserves.

If the wife believes herself to be inferior based on the 'Gender' difference, she would become a doormat for life. If she refuses to play a subservient role to her husband who has been brought up with a patriarchal mindset, things are bound to take an ugly turn. This can be applied to the other differences as well.

Differences in 'Status' create very strong divisions which are extremely difficult to overcome. 'How do we treat people who are much lower than us financially?', 'Do we treat the people who work for us fairly and courteously?', 'Are we grateful to them?' 'Do we have the courage to treat them as the members of our own family or do we let financial differences dictate the way that we treat them?' Nobody can claim perfection in this regard.

From the reports of Near Death survivors, an important attribute that earns us favor in God's eyes, is the way we treat our less fortunate brethren.

Financial status should never come in the way, of forming lasting relationships with people who assist us. These are the challenges that God wants us to overcome. Being placed in a very superior status or position might indeed be God's way of checking our response towards the poor and the deprived people in the society.

Racial bias is also a challenge to be overcome. The following incident created a sense of intrigue in me, when I was traveling abroad. It was unpleasant to experience blatant antipathy because of my skin color.

Since I have 'Asian' origins, I am light skinned and neither fair nor too dark. I was travelling abroad with my husband in an aircraft, and we had seats allotted to us. I was sitting in the middle seat. The 'aisle' seat was vacant and my husband was sitting on my right, close to the window. I saw a woman walk across the 'aisle' to occupy the empty seat on my left. She did not notice me while moving forward.

When she came close she saw me and realized that I was Asian. Instantaneously she changed her mind and moved forward to occupy the seat in front. This row had white people and she was visibly relieved.

I do not blame the woman. She might even have had her own reasons for behaving the way she did. She was immature and did not realize that God does not make distinctions based on skin color. Everybody has to learn the 'Lessons' that life has in store irrespective of Gender, Status or Color, without fail. She was learning at her own pace.

She was accompanied by her husband, who did not have reservations about occupying the vacant seat on my left. In fact he seemed to be very friendly. He probably wanted to make up for the behavior of his wife and we struck up an interesting conversation. He told me that he was in the business of erecting 'sign boards' for the entertainment industry. I was surprised by the contrast in the attitude of two people from the same background.

Behavioral characteristics are not the same for everybody. We become mature through our unique experiences. It is unfair to judge people who have not learnt the lessons that nourish their souls. In fact, they should be treated with sympathy for their ignorance.

I was also able to meet people, whose Universal love for their brothers and sisters from all over the world radiated and illuminated their whole being. I should mention a good friend who accompanied us to restaurants and musical performances to make us feel comfortable in a new setting. She was the personification of exuberance. She was also exceedingly humanitarian.

The warmth exuded by such people was really contagious. One day while I was traveling in the same country, a small child came up to me in the super market and exclaimed, 'Your hair is lovely.' I did not realize that long hair evoked generous compliments. I had never given much importance to my long tresses, but this compliment made me feel 'at home' in an alien land.

I was also pleasantly surprised because this kind of spontaneous appreciation is not common where I live. Moreover long hair is very common among Asian women. Another incident of the same nature occurred in the super market the second time when a woman came and touched my hair, saying that it was very pretty.

I was touched by her act. I was able to meet many people who had transcended 'man made' separations. Anything that divides or separates is not a creation of God. My faith in mankind was restored because of these beautiful souls.

There is yet another disparity which is very poignant. It is the plight of the unorganized sectors which work for minimum wages. The money paid in return for services, rendered by the unorganized sector of workers in some countries, is dismally low, when compared to international standards. These people are treated worse than animals. Laborers from unorganized sectors work from morning till night in the blazing sun and freezing cold to provide for their families.

Surprisingly, I find the younger generation more conscientious in this regard, than the older. They seem to be more generous in money matters, probably because they earn more, and their standard of living has increased.

The messages that are conveyed by every person that we meet in the journey of life are important to nourish our souls. We are destined to learn our lessons from these encounters. Our duty is to try to be as much authentic as possible with the people we meet. It is easy to identify their roles in shaping our lives, when we are open to learning.

Divine will and Divine timing cannot be precipitated to manifest in our lives according to our convenience. We are very impatient to reap the fruits of our labor instantaneously. We fail to realize that when we become impatient for results, we create resistance against Divine will.

When we realize that nothing can be accomplished without Divine will, peace of mind is inevitable. Surrender to Divine will is a prerequisite for happiness. We should wait for the results of our actions, with the confidence that God is not oblivious to our efforts.

# CHAPTER XVII

## THE PURPOSE OF PAIN

Does pain have a purpose? I would have never believed this earlier. But now I know that pain has a very important role to play, in awakening a person, to things which are greater than life. Here, I differentiate physical pain from the pain that affects the mind. My first introduction to this kind of pain was when my mother was terminally sick. It was a gnawing feeling in the heart, which refused to go away.

Sometimes incidents happen which aggravate our pain. When my mother's leg was amputated, my father was devastated with sorrow. But life had to go on. It was a critical time for him, as he was about to retire. He had to continue his work at the office. My father was not a very outspoken person. He spoke very little. But I knew that he was broken on the inside. He carried his pain like a sorrowful pearl in his heart.

The pain that he was going through took its toll on him. One day he developed a temperature. He dismissed it as an ordinary infection, and continued working as usual. After he returned home from work, I noticed that he still ran a temperature. He climbed the stairs with great difficulty. I noticed that his left foot was swollen and it had become dark. My father explained that it was caused by his new footwear. I looked at it closely and my heart skipped a beat. I felt that it was something serious. We took him to the hospital immediately.

This private hospital was very close to our house. But it was a Sunday. It was noon when we reached there. The doctor who had been about to leave, examined my father's leg. He decided to stay back and operate on my father's foot.

He later told us that a delay of even a few hours would have cost my father his leg. He operated upon his leg immediately because his leg had become affected with 'gangrene.' My father had developed diabetes because of stress, and the wound caused by his footwear had become infected.

It was a very difficult time for me. My son was about to be born. My father had to be taken care off. My mother could not be informed about his condition, as she herself was bed ridden. My mother noticed that something was amiss, when my father did not pay a visit to the hospital for a few days. I pacified my mother saying that he had a minor ailment, and that he would visit her soon.

The doctor himself was very efficient and took very good care of my father. I felt that he was a 'Godsend.' Since this was also the time my second child was born, I missed the support of my loving parents, very badly. A few years later I read an article in a newspaper which reported a doctor's death in an accident.

The victim of the accident was the same doctor who had saved my father's leg. I was very shocked. He was very young and compassionate. My father outlived him by almost twenty years. I felt very sorry for his family. We cannot understand these happenings from the human point of view. The only explanation that we can offer is that every soul leaves the Earth as soon as its 'life purpose' is completed.

Pain can make us unhappy, but it should not immobilize us. Pleasure and pain are the two sides of the same coin. It is natural for us to be afraid of pain. Pain can be used for our growth.

Pain becomes our teacher and it is through pain that an awakening of the *'consciousness'* happens. We are continuously assaulted by the painful happenings of life, until one day we open our eyes to reality and all pretences vanish, as we are shaken out of our dream called life. We know that nothing is permanent in the 'material' world.

Everyone does not necessarily undergo the same measure of pain. Pain is unique for every individual. The purpose of every person's mission on earth is different. It was pain which woke me up to the fact that man is absolutely powerless. We are only the tools of operation. God is the 'doer.' My prayer to God in these painful moments is the following, 'I entrust everything to you. I know that you will give what is the best for me.' It is always wise to trust our intuition. God speaks to us through our intuition, in silence, and when we are ready to listen to him.

Nobody is spared from pain in this world. Buddha was protected from experiencing pain for the major part of his life. But when he experienced pain for the first time, it was so poignant for him, that he immediately became enlightened. To understand what is good, we need to understand evil. To understand abstinence, we need to know gluttony.

The Bible speaks of 'Original Sin' and the Mahabharatha speaks of 'Karma' which has to be atoned for, by human beings in their lifetime. This atonement and the subsequent union with God can only be consummated through pain.

Some people suffer more pain than others. The reason for this difference cannot be understood by the human mind. But God is never partial. Every person's journey is God's master plan for the evolution of a soul. Pain is one of the greatest mysteries of life. One instance where I felt another person's pain as much as my own was when a child was brutally gang raped by many.

It is very difficult to digest such a sordid crime. This crime disturbed me so much that I was unable to forget it. The thought of the child's suffering threatened my peace very badly.

In fact I stopped watching the 'News' on Television after this incident. I realized that listening to the 'News' does not help to change a situation in any way. It is true that awareness can be created by the media. But the victim cannot be brought back to life.

We are completely helpless against such crimes. I meditated upon this during my daily walks and demanded an answer from God. I knew the child was at peace. But what had she done to merit this atrocity?

I was walking under the trees and thinking about this. I heard the painful squeaking of a bird, in the school which was behind my house. It sounded very pathetic, as if it was in danger. Looking around I saw a baby cuckoo being chased by crows. The bird was flying from one tree to another for a long time in the hope of escaping from the crows. I could see almost a dozen crows chasing the little bird.

Finally the bird became a prey to the crows which pecked it cruelly with their beaks, and killed it. I was not able to witness this scene any longer and walked away. God had answered my question about pain. That is, pain is an inevitable law of life. Nobody can escape pain.

That does not mean that those who cause pain should go unpunished. It means that these kinds of happenings are beyond the realm of human imagination. Those who cause such gruesome pain to others, also undergo the same degree of pain that they caused others, after their own deaths. This happens during the 'Life Review' which is God's judgment of human souls. This pain is not physical agony, but pain in the consciousness of a soul. Our bodies do not exist after death and cannot experience physical pain.

Many people who have had the Near Death experience reveal that after death, every soul is guided by its higher soul through many dimensions. Some of these souls merge with God who is pure 'light.'

But after this short respite they are instructed to go back to earth because their purpose on earth has not been fulfilled. When they return to earth they experience all the pain and the sorrow that they experienced before dying. Death is relief from pain.

It is not so easy to remain detached from pain. I realized this some time ago when my husband was diagnosed with major blocks in the heart. My husband belongs to a traditional family where he was taught the virtue of 'sacrifice.' He also taught Social Work in a College.

He always placed other's needs before his own. People love him because of his affectionate nature and light hearted banter. After his recovery from 'Cancer' he was healthy for almost twenty years. Two years back, I started noticing some changes in his activities.

Previously I always complained that he walked too quickly for me, but I noticed that his pace had reduced significantly. He seemed to be out of breath, while climbing stairs and he found it difficult to use the 'Treadmill.'

Like many other men he hated to go for 'health check ups' but I had been pestering him to do so, and he finally obliged me. I secured an appointment for him in one of the best hospitals in the city. We spent a whole day on the tests and finally met the doctor for diagnosis.

The doctor did not mince matters and told us that he suspected that there were some blocks in my husband's heart. But he could not ascertain the number of blocks or the intensity of the situation, until an 'Angiogram' was done. He also prescribed some medicines and warned us that we should immediately report to the hospital in case he developed chest pain. I was very worried and wanted to have the tests done immediately, for the peace of mind of the whole family. My children were also very anxious that the tests should be completed.

But my husband had other plans. He did not believe that he was sick and he decided that he would take only the prescribed drugs for an extended period of six months, until he reported for the test once more.

If the situation had not changed after taking the medicines prescribed by the doctor for six months, then he would have the Angiogram. I tried to change his mind by cajoling and arguing in turns, but he stuck to his decision and we had to wait for six months before he took the next round of tests.

I spent sleepless nights in the fear that he would have a 'heart attack' in the middle of the night. He slept well. Six months passed and it was Christmas. There was a new grandchild in the family and everybody was very happy. But my husband was not very interested in having the tests done because he thought that unnecessary tests were being done on healthy people these days.

I could not do anything more, and I gave up because the problem was taking a toll on my mental health. I surrendered to God and just waited for something to happen that would change his mind.

Meanwhile I had inculcated the habit of spending a lot of time with 'Nature,' which gave me a lot of happiness. I was able to forget my cares when I saw 'Nature' following its own course, in harmony with the 'Universe.' I would watch the squirrels playing and moving about actively on the branches of the trees.

They looked cheerful all the time and seemed not to have a care in the world. Since I had resigned my will to God, I had nothing more to worry and I waited for him to act on my behalf. It was as if I knew that God had a master plan for me.

I always admired the children who played in the school playground which was behind our house. They were very cheerful. The school was an ancient one and had a number of very old trees which spread their branches very far, as if to embrace the children who played there.

I began to realize that these trees also had as much consciousness as I did and I felt very much connected to all living things around me. I could feel a special love springing in my heart for 'Nature' and the whole of God's creation.

I could feel that my perception about 'Nature' had changed recently. The leaves on the branches of the trees appeared more vivid and alive. I could converse with 'Nature' and the 'Stars' and the 'Sky' and I felt blessed by God who created and nurtured them.

Every single leaf of the trees was alive and seemed to represent the awesome creation of God. I prayed fervently to all the good souls of the 'Universe' to give me comfort and protect my husband. I did not know that my prayer was going to be granted according to God's divine timing and not my own.

Days passed uneventfully and everything went on as usual. One morning, my husband climbed a ladder to check the inflow of water into the water tank. He was quite weak and must have felt faint, because he lost his balance and fell down. He was able to get up without any help.

He just dismissed the incident as trivial and continued his daily activities. As the day progressed his pain had increased to such an extent, that he was unable to sleep the whole night. He looked very tired and exhausted the next morning, and his eyes were completely red.

I requested a neighbor, who was a nurse, to check his vital signs, but she did not seem to find anything wrong. I decided not to take a risk and hired a taxi to reach the hospital. We reached the hospital in about an hour and a half. The hospital is run by 'Christian Missionaries' and it was the same hospital where my husband's 'Cancer' operation was done. I felt at peace after a very long time. The doctors scheduled an 'Angiogram' for the very next day.

People travel from all over India to this hospital. It is renowned for its dedicated service. It has a very huge and sprawling campus. A small chapel close to the entrance welcomes the visitors who come for treatment. This chapel provides solace and hope to many patients. The relatives and attendants of the patients can be seen sitting on the wooden benches, praying for the recovery of their loved ones.

I felt hope once more. I thought that nothing could be wrong as my husband still felt very confident that he was healthy. We planned to return home the next day after the 'Angiogram' was over.

## CHAPTER XVIII

## GOD'S OWN NETWORK

The next day dawned and my husband was prepared for his test. He had become resigned to accepting the test by then, because his doctors said that they had to confirm the reason for his pain. We thought that the doctors would advice angioplasty, or in the worst case he might have a stent or two placed in his heart. He was taken to the operation theatre for the 'Angiogram,' and I waited outside for the results.

The previous day had been very tiring, as we were unable to have a room allotted to us in the hospital. My husband was in the 'Intensive Care' and the doors were closed to me. I had to wait outside the hospital. I did not like to use the public toilet available to the visitors, and so I had to control my urges to relieve myself. There were hundreds of mosquitoes attacking every part of my body and two hands were not enough to ward them off.

The relatives of the patients in the ICU had to stay close to the hospital, in case an emergency arose. They prepared to sleep in the waiting room and began to rearrange the chairs. The chairs were huddled into a corner and they spread sheets on the floor and lay down and began to sleep.

Since it was an open area outside the hospital, insects came out of their hiding places at night. The one insect that I am most afraid of is a cockroach and I could see many around me. I had to be alert throughout the night. Whenever I saw a cockroach heading in my direction, I would move to the opposite side. My husband was in a risky situation but this did not change my fear of cockroaches. The irony of the situation 'saddened' me. The whole night I walked outside the waiting room in this peculiar manner.

Meanwhile my husband had been sedated and he was sleeping peacefully. In the morning I dozed off for fifteen minutes, sitting on a chair. A kind security person procured some tea for me from outside the hospital premises, at around two in the morning. Luckily we were allotted a room at around ten the next morning.

My husband was taken for the test at the appointed time. I waited outside the Operation Theater, very sure that the doctor would tell me that there was no major problem. The doctor came out after quite a while. His face was quite serious. He said that an Angioplasty or Stent Placement was not possible, because all his three arteries were blocked.

He further added that my husband needed a bypass surgery as early as possible. It was complete shock to both of us. But my husband was the worst affected. He had never expected this situation, and was completely at a loss for words.

Though I was shocked, I did not feel hopeless. My immediate thought was about the next course of action. My husband decided to have the operation done in Chennai, where my daughter lived. My children and their families were very upset after they heard the results. My daughter and son in law supported us wholeheartedly. My husband's siblings and my brother were very supportive.

We did not know the new hospital as much as the previous one. But my husband's friend had given us a reference to a 'social worker' who worked in the hospital. She had to address the needs of the patients and counsel them. We left to Madras immediately and waited for the appointment of the heart specialist, once more.

Meanwhile a very interesting incident happened to me during my stay at Madras. Indian women consider the vermilion as a sign of a husband's good health and longevity. That night I slept fitfully waking up now and then. When I woke up the next morning, I found a generous amount of *'kumkum'* (vermilion) on my hand close to my wrist. I did not understand how it came there and I was puzzled.

I do not believe in magic of any kind, but that day I had a concrete reason to believe that there are Angels and good Spirits around us, giving us signs and hope. I knew that what the astrologer had told me years ago was completely true. Somebody was surely protecting my husband, even though he failed to take care of himself. My Angel had given me a sign that all was going to be well.

I did not give too much importance to the sign, even though I was intrigued by the sight of the *kumkum*. It was dabbed close to my wrist. I have never used the *kumkum* except very rarely and we did not have any in the house. It was nothing short of a miracle.

My mother used to wear *kumkum* to school every day. She was never fond of 'sticker bindis' which every Indian woman (except those who do not use it for religious reasons) uses these days. A red colored paste called Asha, which was available in the market, was used as an adhesive to stick the *kumkum* powder on the forehead. This paste came packed in small round red boxes.

My mother stocked it as she used it regularly. She would dip her forefinger into the red paste and apply it on her forehead to make a perfect circle. Then, she would open the *Kumkum* box and dip her finger into the powder and apply it exactly over the round area, which she had already marked with the paste. The red *kumkum* suited her very well and gave her a dignified look.

I was very fond of making a miniature round shaped *bindi* with the Asha paste on my forehead, when my mother was not around. It gave me a feeling of importance. These small things were enough to make me happy during my childhood.

I never regretted that I did not have costly toys or gadgets to play with. Parents spoil their children by buying them costly gadgets. They do not realize that they are doing the children great harm. Children who are given costly gifts believe that everything can be achieved by money, and that money brings the greatest happiness in life.

Along with the *kumkum* sign that I received from my Angel, I experienced a lot of *synchronicities* during my husband's hospitalization. The 'social worker' in charge of counseling, who was referred by my husband's friend, was truly an Angel in the human form. She arranged an appointment (which would have taken days to materialize) for us, with the specialists, very quickly.

I had no knowledge about the admission procedure or the Insurance formalities. But she guided us in our steps. She gave us the right information at the right time. This was of great help to us. It was as if God himself had specially designated her to help us. She was a part of his Master Plan.

In the previous hospital where the 'Angiogram' had been performed, the doctors had fixed the date of the operation in three days time. It was scheduled on a Monday. But since we decided to get the operation scheduled at another hospital, we knew that there was no chance for us to get the operation fixed on the same date. We waited for the doctor to come.

We wanted to confirm the date of the operation, according to his availability. It was nearly eight in the evening. The doctor had performed an operation and came back to meet his patients, who were waiting anxiously for him. He seemed to be a true messenger of God. He was very kind and explained the details of the procedure, although he was very tired. I realized that I visualized him as a representative of God because of his kindness and his professional etiquette.

The 'accusation' that doctors work for money, and that they prescribe tests and conduct surgeries without reason, is not true. Though this experience was true in my mother's case, it is very unjust to condemn every doctor as unscrupulous, because doctors play a very sacred role in our lives.

They spend very long hours at work. There is a possibility for doctors to get infected by their patients because of contagious diseases. There is also a lot of risk involved in the procedures that they perform.

In my experience ninety nine percentage of doctors, who treated my family members in various circumstances, were exemplary and extraordinarily kind. This specialist was also very kind. He pronounced the same diagnosis that we had received from the first hospital, and fixed the day of the operation. It was on Monday, the same day that the operation had been scheduled to be performed in the first hospital.

To me this was much more than a coincidence. It was a 'miracle'. I could feel the power of God, synchronizing the happenings. I knew that there were a lot of *synchronicities*; because everything was happening at lightning speed, leaving no time for speculation. It was as if everything had already been arranged and we just had to follow the schedule which God had already planned for us.

God was doing everything for me. He was moving the mountains for me. He had sent me Angels and signs to give me hope. I had already surrendered everything to him and I did not feel worried about my husband's recovery, because he was in charge. All the *synchronicities* that occurred continuously removed every trace of worry that had been on my mind. I knew that we were safe. I felt engulfed by God's unconditional love.

The doctor pronounced that my husband was very lucky because he was not diabetic. After his admission, I noticed that many patients who had been admitted at the same time as my husband were not able to have themselves operated upon, because of the severity of the 'complications' that they were suffering from.

I remember an aged couple who were staying in the room next to ours. The husband, who was the patient, had a kidney problem and the doctors were trying to bring down his 'creatinine' levels so that the surgery could be performed without any risk. His family members were worried, and were praying fervently for him.

His wife constantly entreated me to pray to God. She did not mind that we practiced a different religion. All 'separations' which have been created by man, for his own selfish reasons become useless in times like these, when a person's life is in danger. The doctors were able to finalize the dates of his surgery only after a fortnight, because of his condition.

My husband's operation was completed on the scheduled day. I was not allowed to see him for a day. I am truly sorry for the patients who have to undergo bypass surgery because of the excruciating physical pain which they suffer.

The next afternoon I was able to listen to my husband's voice on the phone. He was suffering from terrible pain and he was able to speak only a few words. I knew that he had to endure it because it was inevitable. The 'counselors' did their rounds every day, and they informed the caretakers about the condition of the patients.

The caretakers were not permitted to meet their relatives the day after the surgery, as the patients were still in a critical condition. So, the caretakers were allotted a stipulated time to meet the 'counselors' and learn about the condition of their relatives. The 'counselors' assured me that my husband was on his way to recovery, and that if everything went on as planned, he would be shifted to his room the next day. I met the social worker who had assisted us and thanked her for helping us in so many ways.

We had never met her before. But her dedication to the cause of helping people was remarkable. I experienced God's presence in her kindness and gentle approach. She was a part of the 'network' that God had arranged for me.

There were many people in the network, including my daughter and my son in law who supported us. My son and daughter in law live abroad and they too supported us warmly. But the best support I received was from God himself. How lucky I am to have God as my champion!

# CHAPTER XIX

## IS GOD REVENGEFUL OR MERCIFUL?

That morning, my husband was shifted from the Intensive Care to the private room. He was unable to move or get up on his own. He could not turn or lie on either side, because his rib cage had been cut during the surgery and it caused tremendous pain. The other patients who had been operated recently were also in a similar condition. The pain was unbearable.

I had to lift him very gently with my hand supporting his back, to make him sit on the bed. That night he continuously groaned in agony, and I shed tears of blood. I tried to console him saying, 'Please don't worry. It will be alright.' He replied, 'The pain is intolerable.'

Patients were not encouraged to take too many painkillers because they had a harmful effect on the kidneys. The dosage given to him was not enough to mitigate his pain.

The night that he was shifted to the private room was a very remarkable one. I had just switched off the light before two minutes, hoping that he would go to sleep. He was groaning in pain. I was also very unhappy because of his pain and tried to comfort him with my words.

As we were talking, my husband felt a hand on his shoulder touching him gently, as if to comfort and reassure him. I was lying on the couch to his left and he remarked, 'I feel somebody touching my shoulder and comforting me.' It was a very beautiful moment for both of us, in spite of the pain and the difficulties that we had faced for the past few days. His friend, who was very close to him, had passed away a few days earlier, and my husband thought that his spirit had come to console him, in his pain.

But I think that it was his Angel who was by his side that had comforted him. Maybe both of us were right, because a person who has left this world for another has already become God's messenger.

It is a beautiful experience to be comforted by a 'messenger' from the spiritual world. When people reach the peak of pain, events of this kind become possible. But this does not mean that his pain stopped immediately. For two months after the operation, my husband suffered terrible pain. Then the pain reduced gradually. My husband required my help during this time, after which he recovered slowly.

The hospital provided excellent treatment and people from abroad suffering from heart ailments were admitted there. A woman from 'Nigeria' had accompanied her mother for treatment. Her mother had heart disease, and felt breathless most of the time. They became very friendly with us. We would share our experiences.

She told me that her mother could not afford to be treated in 'Nigeria' because medical expenses were very high there. She was perfectly satisfied with the treatment given at Chennai. Chennai was previously known as Madras. Chennai is developing quickly as a venue of 'medical tourism.'

It is surprising that human beings still insist on ideas based on 'separation' when humanity transcends all barriers. A woman from 'Nigeria' is treated in India because of humanitarian concerns. We may argue that money plays an important role in health care, but at the same time it cannot be forgotten that there is a long waiting list of patients in our own country waiting to be treated.

Many heart transplants and complicated operations are performed in India for patients from neighboring countries. There are no barriers for humanitarian causes. Conflicts are induced by people with vested interests, for selfish reasons.

The hospital experience transformed me radically. Though many events had happened in my life to offer me support, at difficult times, I had always assumed that everything had been achieved, partly through my effort.

I realized then, that nothing is possible without God. This was a major 'eye opener' for me. Earlier, the focus had always been on me, rather than on God whenever there was a favorable situation in life. I felt victorious. But my perspective changed completely after this.

I realized that God had been trying really hard to get to close to me for a long time, and I had not responded to his call. I practiced my religious duties but always thought that I was the 'center' of my life. I understood that God is the center of our lives.

It took the whole of my life experiences to hear him. He had to send me a lot of messages, and even 'miracles' to wake me up. Finally I was an 'Awakened' person.

As long as I was trying to convince my husband, and debating with him to undergo treatment, I was creating a lot of resistance against God's plan. But, as soon as I surrendered my will to God's will, my prayer was answered, at exactly the right time which was the best for me.

My frequent prayer was, 'I implore all the good spirits and Angels to help me.' And God sent his legion of Angels to help me. I may sound too dramatic, but this is the sheer truth of my experience.

I now realize that God lives within me. It is a beautiful feeling. As a child, I had often wondered, 'How can God keep track of the millions of his creations and protect them?' Now I know the answer very clearly. It is very easy for God to keep track of every single being, because he is 'within,' every living organism, and not 'without.' Man searches for God, everywhere except 'within.' This causes disillusionment. He feels forsaken and abandoned. What an irony!

Great philosophers and mystics such as 'Rumi' convey the message that God lives within us, and we can listen to him, but only when we silence the voices of the world. The endless chatter of the material world creates greed and disappointment.

I realized that God pervades my whole being and every single being and organism in the Universe. He has filled the Universe with 'consciousnesses,' in the hope that humankind will evolve slowly and rise to a higher level of 'consciousness' together. But sometimes we don't have the courage to accept the 'miracles' that happen to us. We prefer to think of them as mere coincidences. Life becomes 'simpler' that way and we feel free to continue pursuing our materialistic aspirations.

Recent researches reveal that 'water' has consciousness. The differences in the 'consciousness' levels of water have been studied under a microscope. The results are very interesting. Water responds to positive and negative emotions and words accordingly. These experiments reveal that water takes on a 'beautiful' shape when something positive is said, and becomes 'disturbed' and unclear when we utter negative words.

But how do we treat water? Do we misuse our water resources? Considering the fact that water has a consciousness of its own, and is one of the basic necessities of life, how can we try to preserve it? Water is one of the most abused water resources. It has to be used sensibly. This resource, which was God's free gift, once upon a time, is now sold for money. In many countries rain water is not preserved and it reaches the sea. In these same countries which do not implement suitable policies to preserve water, people in remote impoverished areas, suffer scarcity of drinking water and have to travel long miles to get it.

It has already been predicted that wars may arise in the future because of scarcity of water. But these warnings are ignored. How insensitive can we be? Can we blame God for the problems that we face because of our insensitivities?

World Leaders are more concerned with their struggle for 'power' and egoistic satisfaction. Our Ego stifles the voice of God within us. As the Ego becomes louder, the voice of God cannot be heard, and dies out.

Does Religion make the world a better place to live in? Religions help us to distinguish between the 'good' and the 'bad' in our lives. Without Religion, the Earth would be in a greater mess than it is now. All Religions and Religious leaders promote good values without which we would be 'lost.' Religious leaders are the 'messengers' of God. They are the Prophets of this world.

But we are aware that wars have been waged over religion! Crimes and murders have been committed because of religious beliefs! How can one defend the atrocities being committed in the name of religion? Religions can coexist without claiming superiority. 'Hierarchy' and struggle for power makes Religion meaningless.

Religions should preach God's love. Sometimes, human beings portray God as 'revengeful' because they want to promote an orderly world where everyone is perfect. The Bible says, 'Judge not, and you will not be judged; condemn not, and you will not be condemned; forgive, and you will be forgiven.' God is never vindictive. There is no need to fear him. We have always been taught to judge ourselves for everything we do, beginning from the smallest faults in our lives.

We have been taught to believe that God is revengeful. How do we reconcile with the idea that the same God who preaches mercy and who commands us to forgive unconditionally will punish us with the fires of hell? Many religious teachings have been misinterpreted by human beings, for gaining control over the masses.

But if God is merciful and forgives everybody, how can he do justice to the victims of various crimes? Do criminals go scot free? These are interesting questions. The 'Life Review' faced by souls, after death, which is a part of the experience of every Near Death survivor, answers this question. During the Life Review, every soul is shown a review of all the incidents that happened in its earthly life. Here every soul receives its judgment.

After the life review, every soul is guided by an Angel or a higher soul. Those who are condemned with causing great harm to their brethren, face a difficult journey in their subsequent lives.

Forgiveness is the basic tenet of Christianity. But conflicting views are promoted by people who do not understand that mercy is the foundation of true Christianity. A person of faith becomes puzzled by these contradictions. Some fundamentalists preach about the fires of Hell which are ready to engulf us immediately after death. According to them, God becomes an agent of revenge.

This creates fear of God rather than Love of God. Man withdraws from God's presence, because of feelings of guilt. When we are burdened by our guilt feelings we cannot speak to the God who lives within us.

Does God also live in the hearts of thieves and murderers? Yes. He does. But they have succeeded in stifling his voice to the point of extinction. They are deaf to his entreaties. They have a long way to travel in their journey towards him.

Our 'Free Will' is a gift of God that allows us to make various choices on earth. We have to take responsibility for the choices that we make. Some listen to their 'inner voice' and make the right choices while others ignore the voice within and make the wrong ones. People who sin against others are those who disregard their inner voices.

A person who feels unworthy cannot reach God. When we start loving the God 'within' we will not indulge in profane actions that would hurt the sacred space within us. The choice is with us. Only we can allow God to become our best friend.

# CHAPTER XX

## STAYING IN THE PRESENT SOLVES RELATIONSHIP ISSUES

What does staying in the present mean? It means that we should stop being prisoners of our past and live in the present. It is not always easy to stay in the present. Events that happen every day have the potential to transport us into the past or catapult us into the future. But the 'past' does not exist except in our minds. There is no use in thinking about the 'future' until it arrives. The trick is to be aware that we deserve to enjoy every moment in the present, relish it and enjoy its flavors.

According to Near Death research, time does not occur in a 'linear' sequence in heaven. The past, the present and the future are experienced simultaneously. That is why people who come back after 'crossing over' to the other realm, find it difficult to explain the phenomenon of time in ordinary language. Anything that is man- made and artificial has limitations, and language is insufficient to explain the surrealistic nature of heaven.

Why is staying in the present so important? Staying in the present helps us to reduce anxiety in our daily activities. Imagine being caught up in a 'traffic jam' and being unable to move your vehicle while you are on your way to the office. Not a pleasant experience at all! Does it help to swear about it? Definitely not!

Swearing at unpleasant situations is a reaction from the Ego which likes to feel that it is in control. The Ego feels insulted and helpless in this situation and swearing is the only remedy available to it. But this does not achieve a positive result.

Why does the mind find it so difficult to remain in the present? It is because it connects the present with various instances in the past. It imagines various scenarios as a result of being late to the office. It evokes memories from the brain about the past, where experiences have been stored. We may have been reprimanded by the boss for having been late to work, in the past. This has an influence on our minds in the present, and we imagine that this will happen again. This is how we become prisoners of the past and the future. But we are not aware of this.

Unless a person is a habitual late comer, the situation need not really create a sense of panic or tension. Instead, it can create a sense of acceptance of the 'inevitable.' This applies to all situations, whether it is a simple matter or a matter of great importance. It is not easy to always be in the present, without connecting it to the past or the future.

When we start truly believing in Divine Timing and Divine Will we realize that things do not happen according to our plans. We then start accepting the inevitable. It does not mean that we should not try to seek new solutions, but it is better not to get frantic about it. Every problem gets solved in its own time. Anxiety arises because we expect solutions immediately.

Staying in the present helps to solve relationship issues. When a couple has a problematic relationship history, the events of dissatisfaction get piled up in memory. Even when the husband or the wife is not in the wrong, the piled up history ignites tension under the slightest provocation. On the other hand, if the past is ignored, the incident can be considered as a 'single incident' and the reaction will not be dramatic.

It takes constant practice and meditation to stay in the present. But if this awareness sets in, it is comparatively easier to stay calm, instead of exploding at the slightest hint of a 'disagreement.' Great philosophers urge us to remain in the 'present,' so that we are always conscious of our reactions. If the situation is very serious or beyond control it is better to move away from the situation.

Relationship problems also occur because one of the two partners in the relationship desires to change the other. Change cannot happen unless it happens internally. It is a conscious choice made by a person for his own benefit. If a person has a problematic area which needs improvement, it can only be done by creating awareness in him, and not by blaming him. The Ego plays an important part in deciding whether to make changes. If the Ego believes in being superior, it will not accept change, even if it knows that change will yield positive results.

Every human being's behavior is the result of a unique combination of ideologies of his parents and exposure to his environment. Each believes that his views are perfect, since he has been practicing it throughout his life.

Differences crop up between a husband and wife because; each has been raised by a different set of parents. If the parents of both have raised their children in a similar fashion the differences might be lesser. As a result of these differences expectations differ. These expectations keep building up in the consciousness of the couple.

If one partner fails to measure up to the expectations of the other, problems occur. Sometimes the partners may not realize their faults or refuse to acknowledge it because of Ego or Gender oriented thinking. They might believe that their partner is making unreasonable demands.

This situation cannot be changed immediately. It requires a lot of hard work and effort. Each partner has to give up the impulses of the Ego and make an examination of the inner self. If a change is forced, it will not yield positive results. It would be better for the couple to forget their past 'conditioning,' and change their actions according to the current situation in which they live.

## CHAPTER XXI

### THE AWAKENING

The Awakening is a very difficult process and it can happen only after a person has experienced a lot of pain in life. Awakening means 'Enlightenment.' When you are completely 'awake' you forgive everybody because you understand every person's point of view. When you are 'awake' you hold no grudges against people who have hurt you through their judgment and harsh words.

When you are 'awake' you are strong in the knowledge of who you are, and don't inflict judgments upon yourself. You know that only when you are able to love yourself unconditionally, you can really empower yourself to love others. Without respecting and loving yourself, loving others is not possible.

I realized my Awakening when God touched me through his miracles and synchronicities. When my husband was recuperating from his illness there were visitors to see him, to cheer him up, and very close friends came to visit him. One family, which was very close to us all along, also paid us a visit. I was extremely happy to see them because they had helped us in different ways and I felt obliged towards them.

I knew that I could not repay them for their love. Yet I wanted to give them something. Gifts were of no value to them. It was not a matter of 'value' but a token of 'love.' I wondered what I should give them.

My daughter in law had presented me a pair of shoes when she visited us. But it was size seven and it did not fit me. I wondered whether I could present this pair of shoes to my friend. They were very simple 'walking' shoes.

I did not know my friend's shoe size. I brought them out and asked her to try them. She exclaimed in surprise when she saw the shoes. They were 'black' shoes. She told me that she had wanted to buy black walking shoes. She had also included it in her shopping list. She had stored the picture of the pair of shoes that she had wanted to buy, on her mobile phone.

The picture of the pair of shoes on her phone was strikingly similar to the pair that I presented her. She had been planning to buy the shoes the next day. I asked her to try them on. They fitted her exactly. I was thrilled. Though the shoes were inexpensive the *synchronicity* was very striking.

Since I was experiencing quite a number of these *synchronicities* after our hospital visit, I had almost started looking forward to them. It was fantastic to have a number of *synchronicities* happen at the most unexpected moments. Another incident of a similar nature happened, a short while later.

While travelling abroad I visited super markets and picked out small objects of interest which I could use at home. I collected soap dishes, kitchen utilities, bed sheets etc. But every time that I visited the super market, I was always invariably drawn to the shelf which displayed 'air fryers.' They looked simply beautiful. I was not very sure that I would have enough space in my suitcase for an 'air fryer.' I returned back home without buying it, but still with a small longing in my heart. I presumed that it was not meant for me. I did not mention this to anybody.

Almost six months passed before my son and his wife paid us a visit. They brought us the most beautiful presents. Only one box remained unpacked, and I asked my son what it was. He replied that it was an 'air fryer'. I could not believe my own ears. He did not understand why I became so excited after he made this announcement.

I was thrilled beyond words. I told him that I had been longing to buy it for quite some time but somehow I had not been able to buy it for various reasons. I was stunned that he had bought it for us. I thanked him and my daughter in law profusely. The cost of the gift did not matter but the feelings it invoked was priceless. It was a gift from God. So, I thanked him for the beautiful *synchronicity* that he had wrought for me. I felt very blessed.

A *synchronicity* does not happen without a reason. It is God's way of letting you know that you are aligned with the consciousness of God. Another beautiful *synchronicity* happened some time later.

I visited the church for a memorial service held for a close family member. After the service was over, we returned home for lunch. This was arranged by the family of the deceased. I was engaged in a conversation with a young woman who was closely related to us.

She had recently constructed a house. I was interested in knowing the details of the construction. Our house was also nearing completion and I thought that I could learn from her experience. I asked her to show me the pictures of her house. She said that she had stored it on her mobile phone.

She looked for her mobile phone and realized that she had left it in the church. She had placed it on the pew of the church while she knelt down, and had completely forgotten about it. We rushed back to retrieve it. Luckily the church had been locked immediately after the service. We explained the situation, and the caretaker opened the church for us. If I had not asked her for the pictures she would not have missed her phone for some time.

Luckily she found her phone in the same place that she had left it and she was very happy. I was amazed by the *synchronicity* of the incident, and thanked God for helping me to be an instrument of help.

Sometimes a *synchronicity* also happens to facilitate making amends. Sometime back I hurt a friend by making a rude remark against her. I do not do this usually, but incidents from the past had built a pressure in my mind and had exploded in a very disagreeable way. She was very hurt. I later realized that she was not guilty of any wrong doing.

I had reacted against her because my Ego had been offended. We lived far away from one another and the chances of meeting her were very little. But, I was shocked to meet her twice and at the most unlikely places. I met her in a hospital the first time. I was transfixed because it was the last place where I expected to meet her.

I did not have the courage to speak to her and the chance was withdrawn. She did not see me and moved away. It was an opportunity given to me for undoing my wrongdoing. I missed it because of my cowardice.

I met her again at a wedding a few months later. It was as if the two meetings were arranged on purpose. I did not have the courage to apologize to her both the times. I tried to speak to her but she refused to speak to me. I understood that these *synchronicities* had occurred, to give me a chance to ask for forgiveness. But I was not able to make use of them.

We consider events of these kinds as 'coincidences' and fail to make use of them for our good. Only when they are repetitive in nature, do we understand that it is God's way of communicating with us. His knowledge cannot be comprehended by the human mind. He can choose the most unworthy of his subjects to be his tools.

Instead of dismissing them as coincidences, if we focus our attention on these incidents, they transform our lives and make us more spiritual, as we become witnesses to God's action. God does not perceive with human eyes. It is a wonderful feeling to be chosen by him, and he chooses everybody. Those who suffer a lot during their lifetime can feel assured, that they will be comforted for eternity.

My 'Awakening' revealed to me that God's love is universal. He is not apathetic to our sufferings. He has a plan for each one of us which flows from his infinite wisdom. Our souls do not die. They exist forever and there is life after death. Our earthly life is just a dream when compared to the eternal life that is waiting for us.

# CHAPTER XXII

## GOD AND NATURE

There was a landlord who had beautiful orchards and fruit bearing trees. He was very proud of his orchards as they had the best fruit bearing trees. A wide variety of *flora* and *fauna* flourished in his orchards. He loved his orchards. He also had a number of workers who took care of them.

Once, the landlord had to travel overseas on business and he entrusted his orchards to the care of his workers. He told them to nourish and care for the trees as he did. He also told them to fulfill their own needs from the orchards' produce. There were sparkling streams and wonderful birds which sang in his gardens.

The workers were good. They took care of the orchards well. Some time passed. One of the workers felt that he worked harder than the others, and that he deserved a greater share of the produce. The others disagreed with him. So they decided to divide the land among themselves. Each one had to take care of the land allotted to him. There was peace for a while.

The second worker sold the fruits from the orchards to outsiders and made profits for himself. He also built a house on his master's property. The other workers were horrified in the beginning, but they also decided to do the same, because they thought they had served the landlord for such a long time, and they felt that they deserved to be rewarded.

Moreover the landlord was nowhere around. They thought that he might even be dead. Their greed and selfishness blinded their eyes and each wanted to have more riches than the others.

They did not take care of the orchards but went about their own business. The birds dwindled in number. The sparkling streams lost their sparkle and the fishes died. The birds stopped chirping their happy songs.

The landlord returned to his town and he was shocked. The workers did not receive him well. They protested against him and said they deserved more returns for their labor. They blamed the landlord for all their troubles.

Should we hold the landlord guilty for trusting his workers? He had always wanted the best for his workers. But 'selfishness' and feelings of 'separation' divided the workers and their peace was spoiled.

This is an analogy. We, the human beings who inhabit the earth are the greedy workers. Our focus has shifted from 'contentment' to 'avarice.' Our needs are killing the planet. But we are ignoring the symptoms. We are very careless about our resources and have taken them for granted. No other organism transgresses the rules of nature as much as we do. Even insects follow the course of Nature.

Bees perform the 'waggle' dance to indicate the distance between their hives, and the patches of flowers which yield nectar and pollen. All the birds on our planet are familiar with the climatic changes and migrate accordingly. They follow their intuition. We are the only living beings in the planet who ignore the Ecosystem. In addition to endangering ourselves, we also endanger all the other living organisms. The use of hazardous chemicals has increased to alarming proportions. We use chemicals everywhere and for everything.

Think about the variety of 'detergents' that are available on the shelves of a Departmental Store. All these chemicals are absorbed by the soil and cause pollution. These chemicals cause us great harm when they are used continuously.

The colorful attractive display of a variety of products in the super market is very pleasing to the eye. But they all arrive in plastic containers. These cause a lot of pollution and spoil the atmosphere of our planet. Do we believe that we can exist after destroying the rest of creation?

Our political leaders are not interested in educating us about how to reverse these processes, because they are more concerned about their vote banks. They do not want to spread awareness against 'consumerism' because they know that they will become unpopular among the masses. The leader of every country takes pride in promoting consumerism, and 'materialism' is the 'mantra' which fills the vote banks.

Today we stand at the threshold of a major discovery. Contrary to the opinions of some of the greatest scientists in the world; we now know that God exists. He is pure light, timeless, infinite and true wisdom. He does not differentiate between the rich or the poor, the intelligent or the retarded, the famous or the ordinary, the religious or the non religious as long as we adhere to the values of not hurting our brethren through our words or deeds.

Science and Religion are moving closer, more quickly than we imagined. Science no longer challenges God's existence. God is the rich landlord who has given us this beautiful Earth in the hope that we will coexist with nature.

Do we reciprocate his love? Man's aspirations and greed have led to his downfall. His selfishness that led him to amass, swindle and cheat has put him to shame. The beautiful Paradise that God created for us lies in ruins.

Our Earth has been polluted so much that we cannot breathe fresh air. Many people do not have access to clean drinking water. What God created in plenty for everybody to enjoy, has been accumulated by the minority. The world revolves around the rich minority. People are not respected for their worth as individuals, but respected because they are rich.

This has continued throughout the history of man and we have almost reached the climax. Nature is being destroyed for man's convenience. Nature has not been able to withstand these brutal attacks. Our misdeeds are causing a 'boomerang' effect and destroying us through natural calamities. We predict doom, death and disaster without knowing that we have brought it upon ourselves.

Probably this is why God is giving us so many reminders to reform ourselves. Science has led us to believe that we are infallible. It creates a false sense of superiority and pride. Scientists forget that Creation is a miracle and cannot be replicated.

Near Death survivors report, that after death, they were able to comprehend all the secrets of the Universe and the process of creation, without any previous knowledge about the laws of science. They were endowed with a spontaneous understanding of the 'Galaxies' and the 'Universe.' This was conveyed to them through simple telepathic messages that they received from God's consciousness.

Human knowledge is infinitesimally small before God's wisdom. We have no reason to be proud. We have transformed God's Paradise into Hell. Our Earth is filled with toxic gases that are emitting poisonous fumes. People in many cities of the world are affected by the bad quality of air and develop allergies and complaints. We are the 'Fallen Angels' who have spoilt Paradise.

# CHAPTER XXIII

## MANIFESTATION/THE LAW OF ATTRACTION

We sometimes think that God is very far away from us. We assume that he will not step down from his pedestal for us. God is always trying to enter our consciousness through our intuitions. How many times have we rejected God's voice which speaks within us, telling us what is right and what is wrong. Do we listen to him all the time or do we tend to make excuses? How can we listen to his voice easily? The perfect way to listen to his voice is through 'meditation.'

We need not spend endless hours on meditation to understand him. We only have to be aware of our thoughts every minute. We have to subject ourselves to constant 'self examination.' Life itself can become a process of meditation, when we examine our actions with an awareness called intuition. Our intuitions never go wrong.

Which is the best time to talk to God? We can reach his network anytime. The ideal time is when there aren't too many distractions. Early morning and late night may be the right time to talk to God, because there is lesser noise and limited distraction during these times. It is better to talk to God in silence, because only then we can hear him speaking to us in return. Otherwise, his voice might get muffled by the voices of the world that influence us.

How do we know that we are listening to his voice and not somebody else's? His voice instructs us to do good and not evil. Is our relationship with God a 'one way' street? Do we expect him to fulfill all our wishes?

The image of God as somebody who grants us all our wishes can sometimes make us frustrated. Sometimes our wishes are not granted. Life takes its own course as the events of our life are already planned before our birth.

We are also allowed 'free will' where we make our own choices. Though we are given free will, we have to listen to our intuition to make the best choices. When we ignore our intuition we make our paths more difficult. We become one with him when we listen to it. Only when we become one with God we can synchronize events with his help and 'bend reality.'

Bending reality is directing the course of reality according to our wishes. Many people who teach motivation techniques say that it is possible to manifest the desires of our heart through our thinking. A lot of self styled 'gurus,' teach the process of manifestation. Manifesting something or bending reality to make our desires come true is not a 'monkey trick.' It is a spontaneous process which happens gradually and naturally.

Just like the purification of gold, human beings are tested and tried in various situations. Finally, we reach a stage where we realize that we are nothing, and that we are completely powerless before God. This is when change happens. Only after this realization, we can become co- creators of reality with God.

During this stage our thinking becomes aligned with that of God's. The path which leads to God is very difficult to traverse.

It is a painful road leading to self discovery. Unselfishness, sacrifice and humility should be practiced to reap the best results. The most important requirement is that we should be completely aware of our own nature. Even if we have lost our way we can enter the fold and be comforted.

It is believed that financial gains can be manipulated by the process of 'Manifestation.' It is true to a certain extent. But it is not easy to make financial gains quickly. I experienced the 'Law of Attraction', very potently when I waited patiently for the sale of my house for three years.

This law makes it possible to manifest our desires in the best possible way and in the most ideal circumstances. This law also depends on total surrender to God and faith in his ways.

In the beginning I believed that the sale would be completed in a few months. I made plans based on this assumption. I was confident of my own prowess. But there was no progress for three years. This period of waiting showed me that I was powerless, and I decided to fit myself into God's plan. This was when the 'Law of Attraction' started working.

I entrusted my will to God's and prayed to him saying, 'I know that you will make it happen in your own Divine timing.' This was the point on which I meditated every day. The price that I fixed for the house was reasonable. I prayed that the buyer should be a person who was worthy of the house.

We had lived there for almost three decades and loved our house. It was perfect in every way. I was fully confident that God would work a miracle for me as he had done in various circumstances. I surrendered my intentions to God

God did not disappoint me. Though it happened in God's timing, I could not have chosen a better timing of my own. The 'Law of Attraction' worked in my favor. Though human beings have given this phenomenon a name, it is God's will and grace that enables the 'Law of Attraction' to work in our favor.

Money is an area of challenge just like various other challenges that assault our souls. Some people have too much money and some have too little. Both extremes are meant to be hurdles which have to be overcome. Money should always be 'handled with caution.'

For a person who has too little, meeting daily needs becomes a challenge. For a person who has too much, the manner of spending it authentically for the benefit of the society becomes a challenge. The way in which these challenges are met by individual souls becomes the basis of their soul's judgment.

Some believe that they can manifest their heart's desires by manipulating the Universe. Can the Universe become God? Is it possible for an inanimate being to show unconditional love? Can it judge people according to their life experiences? Can it frame the laws of life? Definitely not! The Universe can never become a substitute for God.

# CHAPTER XXIV

## HUMAN JUDGMENT VERSUS GOD'S JUDGMENT

We are taught to believe in perfection. We are told that flaws are unacceptable. But there can be no personal growth without flaws. Our flaws are the challenges that goad us to become better.

The Christian tradition teaches that the bad Angels rebelled against God and were doomed for eternity. The Angels became jealous of God and they believed that they were equal to him. They tempted Eve with the 'forbidden' apple. When Eve succumbed to the temptation, she changed the fate of mankind. This can be either accepted literally or understood as an analogy.

Every human being born on Earth possesses a soul. Souls have to undergo transformation through the experiences that they have on Earth. Our souls are consumed by various flaws such as Pride, Greed, Jealousy, Anger and Lust. The purpose of birth is refinement and achievement of purity. This can only happen through experiences which occur in every person's life. Our souls are the souls of the jealous Angels and they need to be purified.

Different souls are in different stages of their journey towards Enlightenment or God's love. All souls cannot be judged on the same basis, as their progress towards Enlightenment is different.

It is reassuring to know that God's judgment is different from the judgment of human beings. God is not the personification of revenge. Rather he is the personification of mercy.

Near Death survivors who are messengers from God have the task of reassuring us that God is merciful and loving. They proclaim God's glory, wisdom and his infinite love. They are ecstatic about their experiences with God. More importantly they proclaim his forgiving nature.

It is overwhelming for me to realize, that God loves me so much, that he has performed so many miracles in my life. It is incredible to know, that in spite of my failings, God guides me on my path to his presence. I know that I am a 'Fallen Angel' who aspires to reach the state of purity that God once endowed me with. And I know that God has my back. All of us can be sure

that 'God has our backs.'

CPSIA information can be obtained
at www.ICGtesting.com
Printed in the USA
LVHW042030020623
748642LV00006B/594